D0954769

healing MYTHS
healing MAGIC

Also from Donald M. Epstein

The Twelve Stages of Healing

healing MYTHS
healing MAGIC

Breaking the spell of old illusions;
reclaiming our power to heal.

Donald M. Epstein

AMBER-ALLEN PUBLISHING, INC.

SAN RAFAEL, CALIFORNIA

Copyright © 2000 by Donald M. Epstein, D.C.

Published by Amber-Allen Publishing, Inc.
Post Office Box 6657
San Rafael, California 94903

Editorial: Nathaniel Altman and Janet Mills
Typography: Rick Gordon, Emerald Valley Graphics
Cover Photograph: Photonica, Inc.
Cover Design: Michele Wetherbee
Chakra Illustration: Yi-Shan Shei

All rights reserved. This book may not be reproduced in whole or in part without written permission from the publisher, except by a reviewer who may quote brief passages in a review; nor may any part of this book be reproduced, stored in a retrieval system, or transmitted in any form or by any means, electronic, mechanical, photocopying, recording, or other, without written permission from the publisher.

Library of Congress Cataloging-in-Publication Data
Epstein, Donald M., 1953–
Healing myths, healing magic : breaking the spell of old illusions;
reclaiming our power to heal / Donald M. Epstein. p. cm.
ISBN 1-878424-39-4 (trade paper : alk. paper)
1. Healing. 2. Medical misconceptions. 3. Errors, Popular.
4. Affirmations. I. Title.
RZ999.E67 1999
615.5 – dc21   99–18203 CIP

Printed in Canada on acid-free paper
Distributed by Publishers Group West
10 9 8 7 6 5 4 3

To the memory of my brother, Roy Victor, and my
mother, Marion Lucille, who planted my feet firmly
in the soil of our culture, nurtured my growth, and
taught me that to find the fruit, I'd have
to traverse that proverbial limb.

Contents

Note: To avoid using the masculine gender exclusively when referring to both males and females, we have randomly used masculine and feminine pronouns throughout the book.

Acknowledgments

Special thanks for the wisdom, compassion, love and wit of my wife, Jackie, for her creation of the book's title, her help with the many facets of this project, and her unwavering support and patience.

With deep appreciation for the painstaking labor of my editor, Janet Mills, the CEO of Amber Allen Publishing. Her guidance, persistence, vision, and perseverance helped birth this culture-bending book.

My gratitude to Nathaniel Altman for editing with understanding and elegance. His insights were vital and germane to the process.

I wish to thank the thousands of individuals whom I have attended to whose comments and questions, concerns, passions, healing, and crises showed me the need for Healing Magic.

I also wish to thank the thousands of doctors, patients, and practice members who have trusted and applied my ideas, concepts, and methods.

Thank you to Daniel David Palmer, Candace Pert, Ph.D., Ken Wilber, Drs. Wayne Dyer and Deepak Chopra, Daniel Quinn, Sondra Ray, and Don Campbell for your brilliant insights into the bodymind and consciousness, which provided substantial nourishment for this book and for my soul.

Grazie "Papa" to Padre Eligio, whose manifestation of healing magic in the lives of so many in his communities is a continuing source of inspiration to me.

Thank you to my very wise and loving father, Carl, for his consistent encouragement and guidance over the years. Thanks to my late mother-in-law, Louise, who loved each child as if they were the only one, and to my father-in-law, Jack, who continues to teach me about service.

A very special thank you to my children, Debra, David, Louise, Daniel, and Richelle, for their love and support and for the special gifts they each bring to our family. And to Alison and John Michael and my office "family" for "holding down the fort" while I travel and teach, helping provide the freedom I needed to complete this project.

Magic is nature unimpeded.

—*The Magical Approach* by Jane Roberts

healing MYTHS
healing MAGIC

Part 1

. . . .

The Power of Myth

There was a time, not too long ago, when our ancestors believed that the sun and the moon, the rivers and the forests, were sacred. The changing of the seasons, the rise and fall of the tides, and other rhythms of Mother Earth were sacred. Through story, dance, or song, all children knew the history of their people. They knew tales of creation and myths of belonging in a world where there was a place for them. Children would beg their grandmother, "Nanna, tell me that story again." Their roles in life were guided by a rich tradition of folktales, legends, and myths.

The word *myth* is derived from the Latin term *mythos*, or story. The prevailing myths or stories of a society are considered its norm or "reality," and our myths are sacred. Throughout human history, people have been ridiculed, ostracized, and severely punished for nothing more than questioning or challenging a "cultural hallucination" or myth of their time. By questioning the myth that all celestial bodies revolved around the Earth, Galileo Galilei (1564–1642) was branded a heretic by the Church, and forced to renounce his belief on his knees before being thrown into prison for life. After a seven-year trial by the Inquisition, the Italian scientist Giordano Bruno (1548–1600) was burned at the stake for questioning the same myth as Galileo, and also for proposing that the sun itself may not be the center of the universe.

Our culture and its stories largely determine the manner in which we experience the world and our place within it. Our stories tell us how we are to live our lives, including how we should relate to others. Stories or myths not only provide a context through which we see our place in the world, but also set the foundation for how our physiology will respond to life's challenges. In practical terms, myths help us interpret and respond to our circumstances, situations, and crises.

Our body and mind — which are so interrelated that I consider them together as *bodymind* — are deeply affected by the myths we accept without question. When our bodymind experiences a new situation or challenge, it resorts to the most familiar story about the situation — the story depicting what we *expect* will happen. If we have a headache or back pain, if our spouse walks out on us, or if our car is damaged in an accident, our physiology responds with a story about how things are supposed to be. Then we match our experience to our expectations. It does not matter if the story is true; our bodymind responds from the place of a deep cultural hallucination, which for most of us means a deep sleep.

Just as the prevailing story accepted by a culture without question is considered normal existence or "reality," that of another culture is considered strange, comical, stupid, or dangerous. We are biased against anything that is at variance with our story. If the beliefs or values we unconsciously accept are challenged, we may react with anger, rage, resentment, frustration, or depression. Often, we will reject an idea or treatment because it doesn't feel good, because it is weird, or because it creates anxiety as it clashes with a prevailing myth. Even when we are told that a particular treatment, practice, or dietary supplement is beneficial for our health and well-being, our physiology is likely to ignore or reject it if the idea is foreign to our prevailing myths.

For example, if an expectant mother in our culture is told about a simple procedure she can follow after her baby is born that will restore lost nutrients, improve her immune system, facilitate the transportation of antibodies to her baby through breast milk, speed up her recovery, and is free of charge, she is likely to say, "Yes! I'll do it. Tell me what it is." If the woman is then told to eat her baby's placenta, or afterbirth, she will immediately respond with "Ugh. That's disgusting! No, thank you!" The woman's mind and body tell her, "It's a myth; it can't be!" It is also possible that her bodymind will declare, "This doesn't feel right to me," which brings up another myth: that something has to "feel right" to be good for us.

When we are frightened, confused, or lost in despair, we often turn to our "myth spinners" to give meaning to our experience. In native cultures, such individuals are usually shamans and other types of healers and magicians. In contemporary Western society, teachers, doctors, therapists, clergy, attorneys, and legislators are among the socially empowered storytellers or myth spinners of our time. Taking its cues from these authority figures, our society then legislates and enforces the prevailing myths to "protect" us from harm.

Consider, as an example, the physician who fails to recommend conventional medical treatment to a patient with cancer. The physician can be prosecuted by the courts for malpractice even when there is no solid evidence that further medical treatment will either prolong the patient's life or improve her quality of life. What is society's real concern? Is the legal system acting in the best interest of the patient, or is it more concerned about maintaining the myths and the supremacy of the storytellers of our time?

Another example is the emotionally charged story of the need for immunization. The facts do not always support the theory that immunization is beneficial. In recent cases of polio, most of those who developed the condition had been immunized. Many studies have shown that the risks versus the benefits of immunization are often questionable. Yet observe the reaction of school administrators, physicians, and legal authorities if a child's parents assert that immunization is not appropriate for their child. Notice also how *we* react to someone who questions a concept or procedure that we may have accepted blindly as part of our social story.

Doctor, I Feel Terrible!

Imagine waking up one day with a runny nose, congested sinuses, and swollen eyes. You are coughing and wheezing, and have welts on your body. With all these symptoms, you are likely to be distressed. What type of health care will you seek? Your choice will be based upon the story the practitioner expresses, and whether it matches your story of the world. We have been conditioned to seek the story of the physician for the physical body, the psychologist for the mind, and a member of the clergy for the spirit. Sometimes we seek help from all three for the same problem. While a religious person will invest great meaning in clerical advice and ritual practice, an atheist would view the clergy's perspective as both ridiculous and useless.

If we seek the advice of an allergist, we may be told that we are the victim of an allergy. The allergist's story provides a reason for our symptoms and a way to neatly categorize them. If we are told that we have an allergy, for example, we can experience the symptoms, and go on living our life as we normally do. Many people are uncomfortable until a doctor tells them what is causing their symptoms. If the allergist fails to give us a diagnosis, we may continue to seek a second (or third) opinion. Once our condition has a name, if someone asks about our runny nose we can respond, "Well, it's because I have this allergy." The story also lets us rest assured that we are normal because others have had the same symptoms. Our symptoms and condition may then be considered "acceptable" for the rest of our life.

If we choose to see a nutritionist for the same problem, this person may tell us that the problem is an impoverished nutritional state, instead of an outside substance producing the allergy. As a result, the nutritionist might suggest a different diet or nutritional supplements. If we decide to see a chiropractor, we may be told that

the messages between our brain and respiratory passages are im-
pinged upon by interference of the spinal nerves. The chiropractor's
story centers around the need for messages from the brain to reach
every vital organ and part of the body so that our life force will express
itself properly. Because attention is focused on the spine, the chiropractor may tell us that a vertebral distortion called a *subluxation* is
interfering with the expression of our sinuses or perhaps our adrenal
glands. We sigh with relief. "Whew! Now I know what is wrong with
me."

　　Still, an acupuncturist might suggest there is an imbalance in
the *ch'i*, or life force, of our body, and that the symptoms are a result
of the blockage of ch'i. The acupuncturist uses a technique to free the
ch'i and we exclaim, "Wow, I sure am glad I went there." Depending
on the practitioner we choose to believe, we will adopt that particular
perspective or story about illness and healing, often to the exclusion
of other possibilities. Someone who chooses to see an allergist would
find it ridiculous if a health professional said, "It's not an allergy causing your symptoms, but a blockage of ch'i."

　　Myths have long exerted a powerful impact on the way we
view health and healing. In centuries past, we were taught to believe
that disease was caused by evil spirits. Typhus was believed to be
caused by dark spirits or evil "vapors," until it was discovered that the
disease was spread by certain types of lice that thrive in unsanitary
living conditions. Today, we are taught that disease is the result of
viruses or faulty DNA.

　　Although we experience an illness through our biology, it

involves our psychology and a strong cultural component that is often overlooked. This idea meets resistance from the modern cultural story wherein we believe our biology to be largely removed from the culture. We have not considered that a significant part of our response to circumstances, including the manifestation and duration of symptoms and disease, is linked to the contextual model through which we view and experience the world.

The Powerful Placebo

The story of "Mr. Wright" is the classical American textbook tale of the power of myth in both health and disease. Diagnosed with cancerous tumors "the size of oranges," Mr. Wright was told he had just days to live. While in the hospital, he heard about a horse serum treatment reported to be effective against cancerous growth. Mr. Wright pleaded with his doctor to administer the treatment, and on a Friday afternoon, his physician gave him an injection of the serum. On the following Monday, Mr. Wright was released from the hospital. He was in high spirits and was no longer waiting to die. In his report, the doctor noted that the tumors "had melted like snowballs on a hot stove."

Two months later, Mr. Wright read in the newspaper that the serum was bogus, and he suffered an immediate relapse. His doctor calmly told him not to believe what he had read about the horse serum being ineffective, and then administered a "highly refined double-strength version" of the drug, which he later reported was colored water. The power of healing was renewed as Mr. Wright's mood improved, and the tumors disappeared again. Over the next two months, Mr. Wright was in good spirits and enjoyed improved overall health until he read a definitive report stating that his treatment was worthless. He died two days later. It did not matter if the story was true or not. What mattered is whether the myth Mr. Wright believed in encouraged or discouraged the healing process.

According to Dr. Anne Harrington, a science historian at Harvard University, a *placebo* (derived from the Latin term meaning "I shall please") is, in essence, a lie that heals. A recent article in *The New York Times* reported several new studies that show the placebo effect at work in different cultures around the world. Smelling a placebo helped asthmatic children in Venezuela increase their lung function by 33 percent. In a Japanese study, people exposed to fake poison ivy developed real rashes. In Texas, a study comparing arthroscopic knee surgery to sham surgery produced similar levels of pain relief. In another study, 42 percent of balding men taking a placebo either maintained their hair or increased the amount of hair on their heads.

In an article published in *Scientific American,* several studies were reported on the power of the placebo effect. One group of patients received surgery to treat angina pectoris symptoms, and enjoyed a 76 percent improvement. The other group, the placebo group, had an incision made and were told they had the procedure performed. The group receiving the placebo had 100 percent improvement.

Studies typically rate the placebo effect as 30 to 70 percent effective. If you consider that "placebo" invokes the power to heal in spite of treatment, all the healing that ever occurs can be considered placebo-related. Yet this marvelous placebo effect is scorned by our society. Imagine your tumors disappearing after ingesting a sugar pill! Your physician, business associates, and even family members may consider you a fool to have healed while being duped. A more appropriate response would be to organize a parade in your honor for having mastered the ability to take an inert substance, along with a good dosage of a story that works, and activate your innate powers of healing.

Choosing Our Own Stories

We cannot escape from our culture and our stories any more than we can take a walk outdoors and escape from nature. We can, however, choose to walk in the desert, swim in a tropical ocean, or observe the force of a storm. Our stories, like our experience of nature, are varied and changeable. If we had only experienced life in the desert, our perception of life and its possibilities would be vastly different from our perception of life on a tropical island. Our expectations for ourselves would be vastly different if we only knew the Earth as a frozen tundra or grassy plain. We are inseparable from the larger context of the world we live in, the people we commune with, and the stories and perspectives of the culture of which we are a part.

During the past millennium, the stories we have accepted as truth are responsible for tremendous misery not only in our personal life, but in the world we have created around us. The sun and the moon, the tides, and our rivers are no longer treated as sacred.

The history of our religious or tribal lineage embedded within the memory of our body is no longer treated as sacred. If our story doesn't support a sacred perspective of the natural world and our place within it, then how can the natural rhythms of our body be treated as sacred? Perhaps it is time to realize that what we once considered a "reality" may indeed be a myth. It is time to dispel our cherished myths, one by one, and implement new stories that can set us free from the dark spell we have been under.

In over twenty years of teaching health-care professionals and assisting thousands of individuals in their healing, I discovered how important our stories really are. I have come to realize that our capacity to heal is more often affected by society's collective myths than by our personal circumstances, symptoms, or disease. Profound moments of healing on a physiological level are often limited by the stories we have about who we are, what it takes to heal, and how we see our place in the larger scheme of things. Our stories can create the magic of healing in our life, or they can stop the magic completely.

The purpose of *Healing Myths, Healing Magic* is to help you to become the storyteller of your own life; to recognize and empower those stories that help your life flourish, so you can experience a greater level of health and well-being than any previous story has allowed. Your job, as a storyteller, is to act as a catalyst to bring forth a new story — to convert it from myth to "reality." Of course, the path of the storyteller who dispels the illusions of current myths is often paved with rejection and abuse, because we consider our myths to be sacred. But dispelling old and useless myths is well worth the risks!

Like the creation myths of the past, the stories we adopt have a powerful and magically suggestive effect on the way we interpret our symptoms, the way we heal, and the quality of life we experience. True or not, the story creates the pattern that guides the body toward disease or health. When accepted as truth, certain myths not only impede our healing, but destroy all hope of healing. The prognosis we are given by our chosen storyteller has the *power of creation*. That is why we must be careful in choosing the authority figure we entrust with our health and our life. We must choose our stories wisely, because we are more often affected by our prognosis than by the progression of the disease itself. The prognosis, which is a form of myth, can have the power of a prayer in reverse. The story we accept will either enhance or hinder our healing, and what we often attribute to a condition or its treatment may very well be the consequence of the story or myth we believe in.

It makes no difference whether an old myth or a new myth is true. If the old story results in our being predisposed to high blood pressure, cancer, anxiety, a suppressed immune system, and failing relationships, wouldn't it better serve us to adopt a new one? What if the story about ourselves appeared magical, improbable, and outrageous, but caused our blood pressure to drop, prompted us to experience more laughter, strengthened our immune system, and fostered happier, healthier relationships? Would it matter if someone could prove it to be true or not?

I used to be on a search for ultimate truths. Each time I discovered a new truth, I would share it with everyone I met. It was important to me that others shared my passion for my truth of the moment. One by one, however, I found exceptions to each truth. At the center of each truth I discovered a paradox that I could not resolve, so I would search for a new truth to replace it. Eventually I gave up the search for "truth," and now I seek a story or fantasy that works for me and for those around me — a myth that enlivens and inspires me.

Having a healthier, more alive, passionate, creative, and empowered life is a fantasy that I choose for myself. I, for one, believe that all of creation is sacred. I *want* to believe in the tooth fairy, the sandman, the Easter bunny, Santa Claus, angels, leprechauns, unicorns, and all the other magical beings that help bridge the gap between the possible and the impossible. When I look at the faces of children who believe in such magical beings, I see the sense of wonder and awe in their eyes. Identifying with these magical beings may lead, in time, to frustration and even despair, but identification with the possibilities of the unseen magic they represent is the basis for all hope, all religious story, and all healing.

I invite you to entertain the possibility that you are more powerful, loving, creative, prosperous, compassionate, and healthy than you have ever imagined. I invite you to share my personal myth that all beings are part of one community; you are not alone, and your experiences are not in vain. You do not have to live life by understanding it first. Your body is sacred, and only through fully experiencing your biology can you express spirit more fully, and live in a state of grace.

Every culture "sleeps" within its own mythology. If we wish to awaken from our sleep, we must be willing to evaluate the way we are programmed to experience the world, our circumstances, and ourselves. Then we may choose our own stories of the world we live in, and the way in which we will live in it. When we awaken from our sleep and question the stories given to us by our authority figures, we may choose to continue with those stories, or we can create new stories that work even better for us. Choosing our own stories can be a liberating, life-transforming, and empowering experience.

This book explores four categories of myths that affect our health and well-being: Social, Biomedical, Religious, and New Age. As you read the myths and reflect on their underlying assumptions, you can break through the spell imposed by these collective stories. You, as a storyteller, can put a new spin on these old stories, and replace each myth with your own healing magic. At the end of each myth is a brief paragraph designed to help you create a new story that promotes the healing process. This paragraph, or "healing magic," is meant to be pondered, stated out loud, and repeated as often as necessary to dispel the healing myth. The healing magic offers new and exciting healing possibilities not only for ourselves, but for our loved ones.

In the following pages, I urge you to look at the power of each myth and the hold it may have on you. Many myths commonly held today are ineffective or even dangerous when it comes to healing. You now have the opportunity to "awaken" as we discuss these myths and their influence on your health and well-being. Since the power of our belief in a story may help heal us or kill us, let's search for a story that assists in our healing and causes no harm.

Part 2

. . . .

Social Myths

The predominant form of health-care in Western countries, known as *allopathic medicine,* is grounded in the mechanistic, materialistic model of life. The popular myths surrounding allopathic medicine embody several ideas: that we are separate from the world around us, that we can dominate the world through our conscious mind, and that we can manipulate both our internal and external environments to facilitate health.

The primary goal of allopathic medicine is to treat disease by using remedies that produce the "opposite" effect of the disease symptoms. For example, a medical doctor might prescribe a sleeping pill to treat insomnia, suggest an alkaline for acid indigestion, or apply a cold compress to reduce a fever. If you have a minor problem, you need only apply a little treatment, and if you have a major problem, it requires a big treatment. More treatment is better than less if you have a major illness.

Allopathic philosophy also teaches that human beings are the sum of their individual parts. The medical profession has created a specialist for each of the different systems or organs of the body. Each specialist — the cardiologist, the orthopedist, the neurologist, the internist — has a story about the primacy of a particular region of the body in the disease process. These specialists have come to know more and more about a particular system or organ of the body, and less and less about how the bodymind functions as a whole.

If we are frightened about our health, whatever the allopathic physician says to us holds more weight than a health-care professional who specializes in "alternative" medicine and methods of treatment. But if we are not very sick, we may accept alternative methods of healing. Why? Because this conforms to the healing myth that tells us if we are *really* sick, we had better see a *real* doctor, the medical practitioner. This is in spite of the fact that many medical procedures are proven to be ineffective or even dangerous. We will discuss this more in the section on Biomedical Myths.

According to the established healing models based on allopathic philosophy, if we have a physical symptom or psychological distress, our goal is to battle it, cure it, or control it. Unexplainable and uncontrolled expressions of emotion, symptoms, breath, or body are considered problematic and require intervention by a specialist. Once the specialist applies her magical treatment to assist us in achieving comfort, this allows us to continue living our life as we normally do, without making changes in the attitudes, beliefs, or lifestyles that may have contributed to the problem in the first place.

The intellect resists chaotic events or rapid changes. Chaos is acceptable only if we know about it in advance and can prepare for it. We may ride a roller coaster to give us a tumultuous experience, but we know beforehand that our ride into chaos is limited, and is therefore acceptable. If we have a fever for two days, this may be acceptable, or may even be considered "good healing," but if our fever persists for a third day, it may no longer be acceptable. We cry, "This has gone too far!" Typically, we seek treatment when our sickness, disease, or crisis lasts longer than we give it permission to.

Our attitudes toward control and surrender, order and chaos, comfort and suffering, are shaped by our social and cultural myths. Because the conscious intellect or educated mind is considered to be supreme, we try to use the intellect to control our environment and shelter us from unwanted experiences. Comfort and ease are valuable commodities in today's fast-paced world, and technology continues to advance rapidly as we strive to make our life easier and more comfortable. The ability to manipulate our environment, including our body, is considered a strength and a skill worth cultivating. By contrast, surrender to circumstances in our environment, including our own body, is considered weak, ineffective, and cause for suffering. The more control we have over our experience, and the more we insulate ourselves from unwanted situations and feelings, the more comfortable we believe we will be.

Giving birth, once considered a natural process, now requires a specialist to manipulate and control the entire process, while making it more comfortable for the mother. I was born during the

1950s, when most babies in America were born in hospitals and given formula soon after birth. Because this was common practice for babies and their mothers, it was considered "normal" and natural. For my grandmother, however, this would not have been normal at all. Just a generation before, most babies were born at home with the guidance of lay midwives possessing wisdom no longer taught to obstetricians in medical school. Shortly after birth, babies began nursing at their mothers' breasts; infant formula was unheard of. Although breast-feeding is slowly regaining popularity among new mothers, home births are relatively rare because giving birth is often viewed as a pathological condition that is dangerous and to be feared. Many consider it strange and even unsafe for a hospital birth to occur without the presence of an ultrasonic monitor, supplemental oxygen, intravenous painkillers, and other drugs. The safety and effectiveness of these procedures does not support the social myth that considers them "normal" aspects of the birth process.

Like birth, death is also treated in our culture as a pathology to be feared, controlled, and manipulated. Three generations ago, death was considered a natural process shared by friends and relatives in the family home. Prior to passing away, the dying person would have the opportunity to be alert and surrounded by their loved ones. Unlike the experience in most modern hospitals, people died with dignity, their deaths followed by wakes in living rooms or parlors. When my wife's mother passed away, she decided to decline refrigeration and embalming and had her mother's body "laid out" at home.

Some relatives considered her decision unfamiliar and strange; a few even found it insulting.

Our culture teaches us to separate the spiritual, mystical, and incomprehensible from the physical or material aspects of our life. Rather than seeing the mysterious as an opportunity to surrender to an experience without having to understand it, we often insist that the unknown become known. Magic, for example, experienced without explanation, brings our physiology into a state of awe and enchantment. If magic is understood, or demystified as merely "a trick," we close the door to states of consciousness that might expand our limited perspectives, and bring us joy and hope.

Over the past few hundred years, humanity has gradually replaced what is intangible, mysterious, and naturally satisfying with all that is tangible, understood, and often disappointing. Those things that are tangible are considered "real," and those that are intangible are to be avoided or relegated to the arts or religion. Our lives are more about managing superficial concepts based on our cultural myths than about the direct experience of life. In contemporary Western society, we have become addicted to a false reality where our focus on food, sex, work, sensory bombardment, and crisis distract us from experiencing our deepest feelings and fears. The accumulation of material possessions, the quest for social status, and the endless pursuit of a "perfect" appearance have replaced the appreciation of natural beauty, the value of gratitude, and the pleasure of enjoying leisure time with friends and family.

Alchemists are needed to break the spell of our social illusions, and liberate us to a story of the sacred nature of ourselves. It is time to discover who we are, what is real, and what is not. We are not what we do, yet what we do often insulates us from who we are. Denial of who we are is rarely a positive long-term strategy. It is time to allow who we are to shine through all that we do.

In healing, the spirit and natural process of life are primary, and work most effectively when the intellect learns to serve rather than control. Healing invites us to take a closer look at the issues in our life, and to respond to our deepest feelings. Through sickness, chaotic events, and crises, the things that have kept us isolated from our feelings and ourselves begin to fall apart. Although the intellect may feel threatened and out of control, sickness and chaos often pave the way for healing.

Healing is the outward manifestation of our inner journey of discovery. As we heal, we begin to see the magic in our experience, even when we don't understand the experience itself. Incorporating the "magical unknown" into a new story is the hope of this new millennium if we are to reclaim our power to heal.

· 1 ·

healing myth

Healing requires a trained professional
or a highly educated specialist.

One age-old spell, cast centuries ago, has confused the concept of *healing*, which is an internal process activated by innate wisdom, with *curing*, or treatment that is dependent upon others. The spell is part of the dark myth that has obscured our self-reliance, and fooled us into believing that the magical cure comes exclusively from outside ourselves.

The concept of *curing* refers to the condition, whereas *healing* refers to the person. Does your physician really know about *you:* your hopes, your dreams, the stresses you have been through during your life, the impact of your relationships, your traumas, your patterns or "programming" from early family life, or the spirit that dwells within you? Your physician knows about disease and symptoms, and how to alleviate or control them. This can at times save your life, but *only in conjunction with the power of life that is already within you.*

Imagine if you were to cut your hand, disinfect it, place a bandage on it, and look at it in two weeks. It would heal. If you did the same with a steak — cut it, disinfected it, placed a bandage on it, and looked at it in two weeks — it would rot. The same approach was applied to both, but only one healed. Why? The person whose story is to trust the power of life will remark, "Because only life has the power to heal." Life has a power of its own that seeks advancement, unfolding, and expression. Life begets more life.

At the end of this chapter (see page 59) is a chart that compares two diverse approaches to healing. A person lives either from the *Tree of Knowledge* or the *Tree of Life*. If knowledge is supreme, then the intellect is superior to the body's natural biological functions. It follows that healing requires the guidance of a specialist so highly trained that few patients can understand what the specialist is providing them. If healing is desirable, it must put us through hell, and not everyone is ready for it.

If we live from the Tree of Knowledge, our intellect seeks to control our biology and all the experiences that we do not enjoy. We avoid being physically and emotionally out of control; we try to insulate ourselves from certain experiences, especially those that bring the emotions into play in an unpredictable fashion. However, it takes a tremendous amount of energy to maintain the *illusion* of control and supremacy of the rational mind. Much of our life energy is expended in an attempt to figure out the meaning of life, to understand our experiences, predict the future, and insulate ourselves from undesirable changes.

Although highly regarded throughout human history, the Tree of Knowledge is exclusive by nature. In this old model, the more complicated or the more education required to understand a body of knowledge, the more important it must be. The more difficult it is to obtain, or the more we must sacrifice to obtain it, the more highly prized the knowledge becomes. If a commodity or service is exclusive, which means it is intellectually, financially, and socially available to only a small group of people, it stands to reason that it must be of great value.

In mainstream medicine, the more expensive or risky the procedure, the more valuable it becomes. A diagnostic procedure that is expensive and even dangerous often rates more "status points" than a free evaluation that is safe and easily performed. If a procedure or treatment is free, readily available, and appears effortless to apply, it must not be valuable, because this is not the way of the intellect. Terms referring to the diagnosis and treatment of disease are generally in Greek or Latin, which adds an air of exclusivity and makes them difficult to understand. The names given to medications are even more esoteric. Drugs like azidothymidine and zalcitabine are almost impossible to pronounce, and medications given simpler brand names appear meaningless and confusing to ordinary people: Celebrex, Crixivan, and Stemgen, for example.

According to the Tree of Knowledge, a simple herb or other natural remedy that is inexpensive and readily available could not possibly be of value, while a new drug synthesized from a parasite that inhabits the polar seal (and not just any polar seal, but the male albino polar seal) must possess magical healing powers. The drug meets the requirements of being exclusive, expensive, complicated, and rare. The educated mind likes to play the game of believing that such a product is supreme, and respects any service or medical procedure that fits into the same model. We revere specialists who know more and more about a smaller and smaller body of knowledge, believing they must have a better way to solve our problem.

Professionals who adhere to this model tend to be elitist, exclusionist, and generally inaccessible to their patients. A celebrity-like persona with an exclusive address, plush furnishings, and a large staff help reinforce this image. A busy schedule and long waiting list also enhance the practitioner's image of inaccessibility and exclusivity. Yet it is the elimination of exclusivity, and the creation of community by increasing our circle of participation with ourselves and the world around us, that will promote our own healing and that of humanity.

If we support the Tree of Life, we know that knowledge can never match the importance of personal experience. The Tree of Life teaches us that natural and spontaneous functions like vomiting, fever, and diarrhea are brilliant processes orchestrated and delivered by our own biology. We don't have to know the exact function of liver cells to admire the biological function of the liver. We gain wisdom through life experience — through the living of life itself. As a "Tree of Lifer," we seek to express spirit through the body, and trust that our social wisdom will eventually catch up with the wisdom of our biology.

. . . . *HEALING MAGIC* . . . .

My healing is natural, spontaneous, and magical. I celebrate the innate wisdom and ability of my body to heal me. I nurture the magical healing power that is mine and mine alone, whether or not I receive the assistance of trained professionals.

· 2 ·

healing myth

Healing is not always available.

It is late at night on a holiday weekend. You are feverish and in pain, and you want help *now*. At the emergency room of the local hospital, you learn that the specific treatment you need is not covered by your insurance because it is still considered "experimental." You are told that it may be several years before the treatment becomes available, or that the procedure needed to treat your condition is too risky. Perhaps you are told that you are not a good candidate for this treatment, or your physician's prognosis of your condition is "terminal." Scenarios like this one can seem hopeless. It appears that healing is not available to us at such a time.

The truth is that healing is *always* available. While it may be true that the particular doctor, therapist, or treatment we want may not be available, this has little to do with whether healing is available to us. Illness is due to a lack of wholeness and inner harmony in our bodymind. Healing means becoming more *whole*. It means getting in touch with the energy and information within our bodymind that have been separated, isolated, abused, shamed, or denied. Healing includes eliminating some of the physical, emotional, and chemical stresses that have not been dealt with previously. It also includes becoming more compassionate and accepting of ourselves, and calls for recognizing the greatness within us. There are many ways to heal ourselves, and most of them are free.

Considered in this light, it is easy to see that healing is always available. However, if we believe the myth that "healing is not available," and expect it to be true, we may not find the healing that we need. Any belief that blocks our experience of the natural, effortless, free expression of life is detrimental to life and inhibits our healing. Our expectations can block our ability to perceive the many ways in which we can heal. Our expectations influence the outcome of our healing. Use of the word *terminal*, for example — which generally means that the patient is expected to die — can take away all hope of healing. In actuality, what it really means is that according to the doctor's current body of knowledge, and the results the doctor has seen in other patients with similar conditions, it is anticipated that the patient will die. However, two important limitations apply: "according to the body of knowledge of your doctor" and "the results your doctor has seen in other patients with similar conditions."

Many individuals who were told they were "terminal" are enjoying full, healthy lives years after their diagnosis. One recent example of such a person is Michael Milken, the former financier and present-day entrepreneur and philanthropist. Diagnosed with terminal prostate cancer, he was given between twelve and eighteen months to live. Milken took up meditation and yoga to reduce stress, became a strict vegetarian, and abandoned his diet of burgers and fries for steamed broccoli and soy shakes. According to a recent profile in *Business Week*, "Michael has proven his doctors wrong. His cancer is in full remission."

When we hear about patients with so-called "terminal" conditions, we need to ask some very important questions:

Has the doctor been exposed to other forms of care outside his or her body of knowledge?

Has the doctor studied cases of spontaneous remissions?

Has the doctor attempted to treat the condition according to his or her professional training, but not to treat the patient as a whole person?

Was the treatment of the type that potentially impairs the healing process while attempting to cure the condition, such as chemotherapy or radiation?

Did the physician suggest an "alternative" treatment to promote healing, such as stress reduction, wholesome food, pure water, exercise, nutritional supplementation, and herbs that enhance the function of the immune system?

Was the placebo effect in reverse applied? (I cannot overstate the power of the doctor's gloomy expectations upon a patient who accepts the doctor's story.)

Were musicians called to the bedside of the patient to provide music to inspire, uplift, or help the patient relax?

Were psychological techniques employed to help the patient gain a deeper level of self-understanding?

Was the patient treated in an environment relatively free of electromagnetic radiation?

Was the patient free of the negative programming of television, radio, newspapers, and conversations that reinforce the state of mind that may have contributed to a loss of health in the first place?

Was the patient asked, "Why are you ill?" and allowed to express her views on the subject?

Was the patient asked about what was not working in his life?

Was any focus or attention placed upon factors in the patient's life that bring her joy or gratitude?

Was the patient's sense of humor evaluated or enhanced?

Once the prognosis was given, what methods were used to better understand the patient's body, mind, and spirit?

Healing involves the free expression of life, be it through laughing and giggling, deep breathing, or freely moving our body. Although our situation may be challenging, healing invites us to take our circumstances less seriously, and to laugh and have fun. There are countless activities that promote healing: playing or listening to music, making love or simply cuddling, taking a soothing bath, exercising, paying attention to our inner needs, sharing concern toward others, serving others (and being served), praying (and being prayed for by others) are but a few. Breathing clean air, eating good, nutritious food, allowing our mind to focus on new possibilities for our life are deeply healing. Experiencing nature's cycles and our own natural cycles, and feeling grateful for them, also helps us to heal. Finally, by exploring what is sacred to us in our life — be it art, music, chanting, ceremony, literature, poetry, religious scripture, or nature — we enhance our power to heal.

Some of these things, or perhaps none of them, will cure your condition. But healing is always available, no matter what your circumstances — any time, any place, twenty-four hours a day, seven days a week. Healing is available whether you are tired or energized, feeling great or feeling ill, or feeling happy or feeling sad. Healing is available with or without skilled health-care professionals, and with or without medical treatment.

. . . . *HEALING MAGIC* . . . .

Healing is always available to me. The door is wide open for healing to occur in this instant and in the instants to follow. I may choose to be assisted by a health practitioner, or I can initiate the healing process by breathing more fully, touching my body, and allowing it to move freely and express what was formerly repressed. By doing so, my own healing rhythms are set free.

· 3 ·

healing myth

Healing is expensive.

In reality, disease and illness are expensive, and healing is always free. Just as we made a distinction between curing and healing, we can make a distinction between disease and illness. Contemporary medical textbooks define *disease* as an *objectively* verified disorder of bodily functions or systems, characterized by a recognizable cause and by an identifiable group of signs and symptoms. *Illness*, by contrast, indicates a person's *subjective* experience, which may or may not indicate the presence of disease.

Curing a disease, or trying to eliminate our symptoms, condition, or crisis through medication, surgery, psychotherapy, or other modalities, can be extremely expensive. Illness, however, is more expensive than even the most expensive treatments for disease. If we were to place a dollar value on the debilitating effect that illness has on each of the most important areas of our life, including relationships, work, study, finances, recreation, and the overall enjoyment of life, we would be surprised at how important and valuable a healthy bodymind really is.

When we are healthy, we attract new opportunities and possibilities. We have energy to play, to work, to give, or to share with others. When we are feeling ill, our bodymind says, "I can't," and our happiness and good fortune often slip away. Illness brings a loss of vitality and creative thinking, a loss of the ability to maximize opportunities, and difficulty in formulating short- and long-term goals. Illness pervades our entire life; it brings a loss of the desire to work and play, a loss of the ability to maintain satisfying relationships, and diminishes our capacity to enjoy romantic and erotic love. Illness represents not only a substantial loss for ourselves, but a loss of the love, guidance, and inspiration we can provide to our family and friends. Illness brings nothing new, mysterious, rewarding, or exciting to our lives. In healing, however, we experience greater opportunities to be enriched and rewarded in many ways. Healing pays, while illness always costs us.

· · · · · · · · · · · · *HEALING MAGIC* · · · · · · · · · · · ·

The internal process that is mine alone is both priceless and free. Although I may pay for a professional to assist me in regaining my health, the process initiated by me, within me, and through me is absolutely free. I claim my freedom to heal and celebrate my own healing power.

· 4 ·

healing myth

Healing takes a lot of work and requires full commitment.

Healing, in fact, is easy and effortless. Of course, if we try to use the intellect to gain control of the healing process, it *does* require work and full commitment. Healing does not reside in the domain of the intellect; healing is a natural and spontaneous part of life. If it were not, there would be no one alive to read this book. The human species has learned to thrive under life-challenging circumstances. This is how our family's lineage has survived long enough to produce us as its promise for the future. We are the salvation of our ancestors, and each one of us is the hope of future generations.

Ken Wilber, perhaps the world's greatest modern explorer of consciousness, has said that evolution produces greater depth, and "as depth increases, consciousness increasingly awakens, [and] spirit increasingly unfolds." We can say that a molecule has more depth or "purposeful complexity" than an atom, and a cell has more depth than the molecules that comprise it. Likewise, the human body has all the levels of complexity and intelligence of all the organs and systems that comprise it. Our bodymind enjoys greater organizational complexity, a more highly developed consciousness, and an increased potential to adapt to difficult circumstances than ever before.

The myth that "healing takes a lot of work" underestimates our unique ability as human beings to adapt, survive, and thrive, even when faced with extreme physical and psychological hardship. This myth ignores our inherent abilities, strengths, and gifts. If we accept this myth as truth, we may downplay our talents, overlook our accomplishments, and fail to appreciate our innate gifts of humor, compassion, and spiritual insight.

When we become aware of these gifts, and experience our own "purposeful complexity," our consciousness shifts toward the Tree of Life, and this shift is associated with healing. Those who align themselves with the Tree of Life begin to accept their symptoms, circumstances, or conditions with gratitude. They find ways to be grateful for the experience of pain or disease in their bodies, for their healing progress, and even for the ability to feel what they don't like feeling. As a result, more of life's gifts come their way.

We need to remember that becoming ill is what really takes work. The average person spends most of her energy trying to avoid the inevitable: change. Generally speaking, it takes more energy to resist the changes in our life than to surrender to them. Life is meant to be fully experienced. Instead of expending our energy to resist life, we need to fully experience it.

When we attempt to control our life experiences, our body becomes inflexible, and structural impediments begin to appear. Loss of motion of the spine and joints of the body develop as we resist the motion of life. Tension builds up in our bodymind, and inhibits the circulation of fluids in the body, and the natural rhythm and function of our organs. The body then devotes its energy toward building rigid muscular walls and energetic blocks that ultimately lead to physical pain. Emotional distress is also associated with energy that is blocked in any area of the body. These conditions, of course, demand more attention and consume more physical energy than a healthier existence.

Healing is natural and spontaneous, but an inability to experience our body with confidence and trust can hinder the healing process. Our body attempts to heal itself by releasing what it no longer needs — physically, chemically, emotionally, or energetically — but our intellect tries to resist or stop this process. Our bodymind is able to renew and reorganize itself automatically and effortlessly, but this process can be upsetting to our personality. Healing may require us to say things we don't like to say, hear things we haven't heard before, feel things we don't usually feel, and deal with things we have always resisted. If we judge our symptoms as "bad" or "wrong," this also requires a tremendous investment of energy.

Healing is easy, effortless, and natural. The healing power within us knows what it wants and needs. Change naturally occurs in the bodymind as an aspect of its adaptive process. Only when we resist or fear change does a change required by our bodymind involve work for our personality. In healing, the main work is to surrender the urge of our intellect to control life, and to detach from a specific out-come. By surrendering to the natural rhythm and flow of life, we step into the natural rhythm and flow of healing.

. . . . *HEALING MAGIC* . . . .

My healing is effortless and natural. My commitment to heal is a natural process requiring no work or special focus on my part. I am grateful for where I am in my healing process. I commit to my whole-ness because it feels natural to do so.

· 5 ·

healing myth

Healing means becoming more balanced, comfortable,
and in control of my experience.

This healing myth could be called the "granddaddy" of many of
the myths found in this book. It has its origin in outmoded views
about order and chaos that can be traced to the roots of the Tree of
Knowledge.

According to this old myth, success in life depends upon
becoming more balanced, comfortable, and in control of our life.
Small changes are acceptable and encouraged, but rapid, unpredictable changes are to be avoided and controlled. This myth encourages us to seek a life that is predictable and safe — a life in which our
plans never have to undergo rapid change. We are taught to insulate
ourselves from feelings, experiences, situations, and events that we
prefer not to have. When applied to healing, this myth suggests that
chaotic events, disease symptoms, or any situation that disrupts our
daily routine or plans are to be resisted, controlled, or eliminated.

By adhering to this myth, we never give ourselves permission to gain the wisdom these experiences might offer.

Symptoms and disease often have their roots in old, unresolved feelings. They arise when the truth can no longer be silenced or obscured by our convenient and established story. What we resist only persists and grows stronger, until we can no longer keep these feelings contained within a particular region of the body. Disease, discord, and other chaotic events bring us the opportunity to break free of this energetic prison; we are biologically encouraged to "deal with it."

It is unfortunate that we may have to experience symptoms of disease to release the feelings inside us, but eventually, we will feel what we are concealing. A high fever, for example, helps dissipate energy that has been blocked within the body; it increases circulation, stimulates white blood cell production, enhances immunity, and promotes the filtration and elimination of toxins. Coughing and sneezing are dramatic ways by which the body breaks down boundaries in the respiratory system. Vomiting and diarrhea are chaotic ways in which the body releases what no longer serves the digestive system. Pain provides a clear, direct message that tells us to modify our behavior or stop what we are currently doing.

Change is a natural part of everyday life. A loss in life can eventually lead to a greater gain; a broken heart creates the opportunity for an open heart. Healing occurs as we live our experience without labeling it as balanced or unbalanced, comfortable or disturbing, and relinquish the myth that our educated mind knows more than our body's own healing mechanisms.

Joe's Story

Joe was a star quarterback in high school, and made excellent grades in college. Graduating with honors from law school, he landed a job in a major law firm and married his high school sweetheart. They entertained regularly in their upper-middle-class suburban home, and their children went to boarding school. Joe was soon promoted to partner at his firm, and his daily life was as neatly manicured as the landscaping of his small estate.

Although he appeared to be enjoying a perfect life, Joe began to develop high blood pressure, lower neck pain, and degenerative arthritic changes in his neck. He was taking one drug to control his hypertension, and another to help alleviate his migraine headaches. By the time Joe was forty years old, he had already undergone two spinal disc surgeries. His wife, who was living a similar lifestyle, was slowly becoming disabled with multiple sclerosis.

Joe's life remained carefully scheduled, and all annoyances and unexpected events were kept at bay. Everything in his life was seemingly balanced and under control, until a scandal revealed that his father, who was white, was having an affair with a woman of color. This was discovered the same year that Joe's only son announced that he was gay. Then his father passed away. No matter how Joe tried to insulate himself from these emotional upheavals, he could not. Medication could no longer mask his physical pain. Joe felt he was losing control over his life, and his physical and emotional condition deteriorated. At work, he was getting confused and less tolerant with clients. Then one day, after an angry outburst in the courtroom, Joe collapsed in pain.

Joe was incapacitated and confined to bed, and his wife reported that he "cried like a baby" for hours at a time. She soon became disgusted and frustrated with her husband, who could no longer contain his feelings and had "lost his dignity." Joe realized that his life was no longer under control. He took a leave of absence from work, sold his stock and real estate holdings to pay the bills, and, within a month, experienced a breakdown.

The shell that had separated Joe from the chaotic, emotional aspects of his life was cracking. Soon he decided to begin care at my clinic to improve the communication between his brain and the rest of his body. As Joe began to feel all the emotion he had previously denied, he felt freer than he had ever felt in his entire life. He stopped watching television, and began to sing spontaneously in the shower, in the car, and even while waiting in line at the supermarket. Joe's blood pressure dropped, his headaches disappeared, and he regained full motion in his neck. Within months after the breakdown, his body was relatively pain-free. Through the chaotic events of his breakdown, Joe began to rebuild his life and become whole again.

Joe's story illustrates how chaotic, unwanted events can have a positive impact on our life. Chaos and change will often redirect our journey toward greater self-discovery, broader perspectives, and the beginning of new and exciting relationships. Healing is not always what we think it is.

. . . . *HEALING MAGIC* . . . .

I give thanks for the unexpected events that take me from my established course and bring new experiences, relationships, and healing. I take this moment to rejoice in the miracle of life. I trust the flow of life, wherever it takes me, and make room in my day to celebrate changes in my schedule and plans. I am nurtured by change, and embrace both chaos and order in my life.

· 6 ·

healing myth

Healing means understanding what went wrong,
or who did what to me.

To heal, we do not have to understand what went wrong in our life or who did what to us. If a person is recovering from a heart attack, would his recovery be enhanced by trying to figure out what he did wrong, or who did what to him? I think not. Instead, he needs to rest, including his conscious, chattering mind.

The fact is, we cannot know what went wrong or how we arrived at our present situation until we *experience* it with our biology. We cannot see the forest if we are looking at a tree. Likewise, we cannot see the benefit in a hurt or trauma from the place of our suffering. We cannot resolve any problem with the same consciousness that created the problem in the first place. Hate cannot resolve hate, anger cannot resolve anger, and confusion cannot resolve confusion. Resolution can only occur when we move outside the context of the situation that troubles us.

As we heal, we can stand back, put distance between ourselves and our situation, and gain a new perspective. Only then can we expand our awareness and see where we have been. This is why, when we are having a fight with our partner, at least one of us needs to take a break, go for a walk, and gently breathe for a few minutes. After we calm down, we can then work to resolve the situation from a perspective other than rage and fury. Studies in meditation and biofeedback show that when the conscious mind becomes relatively silent, our blood pressure drops, immune function improves, healing is enhanced, and love is more available. When relaxed, we tend to feel more compassionate, more creative, and more connected to the primal web of life.

The shift in our physiology is what triggers a shift in our awareness. Once our awareness shifts, we are able to discover and implement new ideas, but *new ideas do not shift our awareness*. Instead, a change in the physiology and integrity of our bodymind shifts our awareness. Only when our bodymind is ready are we able to receive new ideas that assist us in healing. Until then, we resist new ideas or practices that could have much to offer. When our physiology has healed enough, we even find new ideas easy to implement. Something from deep inside tells us, "Now's the time! I'm ready!" An old adage reminds us: "When the student is ready, the teacher appears."

Have you ever tried to interest your partner in a new way of doing something? It may be an exercise program that obviously works for you, or a diet that he knows is good for him. You think, "Perhaps if I give him one more article on this subject, or a new tape discussing the benefits, he will come around." Encouraging him to change becomes a source of tension in your relationship. Then one night as you lay in bed talking, he tells you that he ran into an old friend who gave him the very book you have wanted him to read for several years. Your partner is excited about the "new" idea, and suddenly he can't wait to implement it.

"What has happened here?" you ask yourself. "Am I losing my mind? Why has he suddenly taken an interest in this book? Does he trust his friend more than me? Did he hear anything that *I said?*" Our bodymind can only receive what is consistent with the consciousness it is currently expressing. Who we are at the moment determines what we can think, feel, and do. When we are healthy enough to make a change, we offer no resistance to those ideas or practices that support a healthier life.

. . . . *HEALING MAGIC* . . . .

To heal, I don't need to understand what has happened in my life or why. I celebrate the miraculous interrelatedness of people, events, and circumstances. I allow myself to experience a new state of consciousness by expanding my chest with air, and placing my hands on my heart. As my bodymind heals, my awareness shifts, and old wounds dissolve into nothingness.

· 7 ·

healing myth

*Someone else has to have healed from
this disease before I can do it.*

"So Doctor, what are my chances? Have others made it with what I've got?" Given the current myths of mainstream medicine, prognoses are often made considering the condition, not the person. Someone had to be first in every arena. Passing down the same road that others have traveled certainly gives us a greater feeling of ease; however, new roads to healing can always be paved.

When we are given a prognosis, the data is most likely collected from patients in a hospital who have been diagnosed with the same or similar condition. The first point to be aware of is that a population of hospital patients is not necessarily representative of the general population. People in the hospital are most likely those who still suffer from symptoms of disease. Those who recover on their own are not likely to be included in the data used for the prognosis you are given.

Doctors often report cases of tumors they discover to a central agency, but there is no central reporting agency that coordinates data on the regression, remission, or elimination of tumors. In addition, when someone heals and drops out of allopathic medical treatment, her progress is no longer in the database of the professionals who submit a prognosis. The knowledge base of professionals is often limited to those who have followed their particular story and treatment modalities.

Hospitals are rarely places where we become empowered in our healing process. Nor are they known to be places where we can discover trust in the human body. Instead, they reinforce old healing myths that further disconnect us from healing magic. Patients in hospitals are generally not encouraged to laugh, touch others and be touched, or eat fresh food. They are rarely given dietary supplements to support their health and to help neutralize the harmful effects of medical treatment. Fresh air and sunlight are rarely available to hospital patients.

Often isolated from their emotional support system, patients spend most of the day and night under some form of sedation, and bathed in high electromagnetic radiation while resting in the hospital bed. A hospital stay reinforces the dark myths that tell us that we are alone and helpless, that our bodies are stupid, and that the only way to heal is to do what a professional tells us to do. The modern hospital is the temple of these mythologies. It is generally not a place, regardless of treatment, where the contact you have with staff nurses and doctors will reduce your stress level, enhance your immune system, allow you to express your inner self, or inspire you to feel joyous to be alive. Yet the population of patients within hospitals becomes the basis for a doctor's clinical judgment as to how we will progress.

Our state of health is the result of a multitude of contributing factors. Emotional issues, how we deal with stress, the existence of a personal support system, and adequate nutrition and exercise all have a powerful impact on healing. Other healing modalities, such as chiropractic, Somato Respiratory Integration, acupuncture, homeopathy, massage, and yoga also affect our healing, and are utilized by many people. Considering that other healing techniques and experiences that greatly affect our life are not included in the physician's diagnosis, little information relative to *us* has been considered when we are given a prognosis.

Finally, it is important to remember that although two people may be diagnosed with the same disease and appear to have much in common, they may have traveled down very different paths to produce their illness. In addition, these people may need to explore different avenues of healing with radically different scenarios on their way to wholeness. Another person may have the same or similar condition and prognosis, but this doesn't mean that her treatment or outcome will be the same as ours.

The doctor may seek to treat the condition, but the condition cannot be separated from the person who experiences it. The condition may or may not be curable, but *the person can always heal*. The power of life flows freely through the body unless it is blocked by a physical obstruction or by the conscious, thinking mind. The power of life flows more freely within the person whose story or myth gives it permission to flow.

· · · · · · · · · · · · *HEALING MAGIC* · · · · · · · · · · · ·

I am a powerful, creative, and evolving being. The power of life that creates and sustains me knows precisely how to heal me. I give my physiology permission to allow this power to flow through me and to heal me. It is okay for me to be the first to have healed in this way. My healing inspires countless others to trust the healing power within.

· 8 ·

healing myth

In healing, to be average is normal, and therefore desirable.

In contemporary Western society, to be average is considered normal. People generally have less tolerance and more judgment of those members of society who fall outside the range of "average." Nonconformists are often scorned and regarded as strange, weird, or crazy. Rather than applauding those who stand out from the crowd for their eccentricities, unique abilities, or unusual accomplishments, those who do not conform to the acceptable standards of society are viewed as outcasts. In fact, our society condones uniformity. By being average or "normal" we can fit in with "respectable society," avoid the harsh criticism of others, and stay somewhat safe and comfortable. Of course, this will be at the expense of our own authentic self.

Our cultural myths tell us to interpret what is unique, special, out of balance, and extraordinary as abnormal. In years past, psychological and emotional breakdowns or other forms of extreme behavior were considered pathological. Today such experiences are viewed by some health-care professionals as part of the healing process, based upon the improvement in a person's condition. As we have seen, sometimes an emotional breakdown enables an individual to resolve traumatic or overly sensitive situations, and may even lead to new discoveries and directions in life. Although society attempts to make everyone the same or "average," life brings out the unique qualities and gifts within each of us. Healing may require that the authentic you, with all of your unique features and attributes, leave the normal behind and break free of old social paradigms.

As in the rest of society, "average" plays an important role in mainstream medicine. If a chemical evaluation of a blood sample reveals average values of the typical person without any diagnosed pathology, then the sample is considered normal. Yet "normal" does not necessarily mean healthy; it simply means that the person's blood readings are in the range considered "average." If you are sick, your body chemistry is going to change as you move toward health. When your body or mind is purging physical or emotional toxins, it may not appear to be average. Every sign and symptom of healing might appear "unusual" compared to where you have been before.

It has been said that insanity is doing the same thing we have always done, and expecting a different result. Likewise, it could be said that insanity is attempting to remain average or normal while expecting our bodymind to heal.

. . . . *HEALING MAGIC* . . . .

I have no need to be average or normal. I surrender the need to fit into the expectations of others at the expense of my own evolution. At times, upon claiming my wholeness, I may look, sound, or "test" non-average. I joyfully celebrate my loss of normalcy, and claim my authenticity, sanity, and health.

· 9 ·

healing myth

Healing means liking my experience
and agreeing with the outcome.

As part of the cultural myth that places comfort and ease before discomfort and "dis-ease," we judge the physical symptoms we do not like as "bad." Symptoms are perceived as unwelcome visitors, or as burglars who have assaulted us in the privacy of our own bodily home. Our pain or disease is considered to be a personal attack on our person. Under these circumstances, it can be more challenging for our bodymind to heal. Let's look at the typical reactions we have when faced with physical symptoms or pain.

First, we judge our symptoms as bad or wrong, and fail to listen to their message. If our back is hurting, what do most of us do? Do we ask ourselves what message our back may be giving us? Do we place our hands on our back, and breathe with the message, moving our hands as it asks us to move? Do we love our back pain for the story it has to tell? Most of us will curse the messenger (the back) and refuse to listen to the message. If our pain causes us to modify our daily routine or forces us to change the way we are living our life, we promptly consult a doctor to silence the messenger, without ever listening to the message!

We do not have to agree with the timing our body has chosen to deliver a message, nor do we have to like or enjoy our experience. What we must do in order to heal is simply *experience the experience* of our biology. It is important to have compassion without judgment or condemnation. Saying "I love you" to a part of our body doesn't mean that we are never inconvenienced, that we won't have to surrender to an uncomfortable situation, or that we never have to make any sacrifices. We need to love the messenger for the message it has to give us. Only as we acknowledge and accept the message (even when it is perceived as pain) can we respond to our body with love and compassion.

Second, we label the "damaged" part of our body or give our condition a name. We refer to our back as "a bad back," our knee as "a bum knee," or our heart as "a bad ticker." This impression of our body is further validated by a professional who places a Greek or Latin translation on the condition, such as osteoarthritis, sciatica, or angina pectoris. Now the name becomes the *reason* why we are ill. We become a victim of our condition, and move further away from feeling compassion for ourselves or the part of our body that has a message to give us. Now our condition is the *cause* of our trouble, rather than the *result* of faulty habits, prolonged emotional trauma, or a toxic lifestyle.

When our focus is placed on the "cause and effect," this eliminates our responsibility for the events or circumstances that might have led to the crisis or condition. If it is "our arthritis," we are no longer responsible for it. Our condition has a home, and it becomes a part of our identity. No one has the right to take "our arthritis" away from us unless we are ready to surrender it.

Once we have given our condition a fancy name, our symptoms are no longer an important signal to pay attention to. Rather than offering a simple message that says "pay attention," or "I am needy," the disease takes on a life of its own, and this engenders anger, upset, victimization, and a sense of failure. Judgment, anger, and feeling victimized set up a situation in our physiology that is counterproductive to healing. If we judge a part of our body as wrong, we can easily justify punishing, attacking, or destroying it. The label gives our intellect the focus it needs to control the symptoms or bombard our body with drugs, surgery, or dangerous treatments.

Instead of judging, naming, and trying to control our condition, we need to adopt a loving approach. If our symptoms are viewed as a signal that we are needy, this engenders compassion and a desire to attend to those needs. Loving involves unconditionally serving, accepting, and surrendering, while remaining whole in the process. Loving calls us to surrender to the rhythms of our bodymind, as well as tearing down walls that keep us isolated as a separate being in the world. It requires that we value our life, our happiness, and our healing more than the false images we project to others.

We are not what other people call us; we are not what we do; we are not our college degrees or other accomplishments. Beneath all these outer images is who we really are. For others to see the real us, they have to look beyond our words, actions, and deeds, and pay close attention to what is behind the outer appearances. I suggest that when it comes to healing, we need to adopt the same perspective, and pay close attention to what is *behind* our symptoms and disease.

. . . . *HEALING MAGIC* . . . .

I love and honor my body, even when I don't like my experience. When physical symptoms or pain arise, I pay attention and accept them without judgment. The messages of my body are perfectly timed for my healing. I listen to the rhythms and messages of my body, and attend to its needs with compassion.

· 10 ·

healing myth

Healing is a destination.

This is another stone in the foundation of an old cultural myth. This myth teaches us to seek immediate comfort and ease through curing, at the expense of healing our bodymind from the larger perspective of our life. Healing is a journey, not a destination. If we view healing as a destination, we try to rush the process toward the goal, without considering what our bodymind and symptoms are telling us. This can lead to much suffering, and result in a chain of destinations that I refer to as the "cure-cause-effect."

Let's consider the elimination of an undesirable symptom, behavior pattern, or disease to be the destination, and the treatment or behavior modification to be the means to our destination. If we define success as "the successive realization of preconceived goals," then to attain success we need a starting point, a clear destination, and a means of transport.

According to what is known as "systems theory," when you attempt to modify a system, short-term results may appear positive, although long-term results (usually due to various unexpected interactions) are often the opposite of what we want to create. In our relationships in general, and with our body in particular, what we do to correct or manage a symptom often becomes the cause of a new problem. Each destination in the healing process becomes the starting point of a new journey.

Consider the example of Mary, who is suffering from an earache and a sore throat. The "destination" is the elimination of the ear infection and the sore throat. The "vehicle" is a course of antibiotics. After five days of antibiotics, the infection appears to be cured, and Mary has arrived at her destination. However, now she has a rash from the antibiotics, an irritated intestinal tract that produces gas, and a vaginal yeast infection.

As a result of these new problems, and being a private person, Mary does not want to discuss her gas or vaginal infection with her boyfriend, and avoids close physical contact with him. Her boyfriend feels rejected, which causes friction in their relationship. This stress aggravates Mary's high blood pressure and migraine headaches. As a result of these new symptoms, she increases her high blood pressure medication, and takes time off from work because of her intense headaches. As she falls behind at work, she loses her job, which further stresses all of her relationships. At the same time, the medication Mary is taking to control her high blood pressure reduces her libido. Due to depression, Mary begins to binge on sweets and high-fat foods, adding to the hypertension and weight. She is then given a tranquilizer for her depression, in a vicious cycle of symptoms, medications, and destinations.

While it may be true that curing sometimes leads to just one destination, it often produces a new problem, either immediately or over time. Each symptom in turn receives its own treatment with different destinations in mind. This dynamic, or the "cure-cause-effect," actually involves a perpetual chain of treatments.

Our healing must include the totality of ourselves, not merely a quick cure for our symptoms or condition. Healing requires that we remain awake and aware as we travel on this journey called life. To view healing as a lifelong process or journey eliminates the need to attain a specific goal within a preconceived time frame. It also reminds us that whenever we embark on a journey toward health, we are going to encounter hills and valleys, roadblocks and traffic jams, as well as more pleasant rest stops along the way.

· · · · · · · · · · · · · *HEALING MAGIC* · · · · · · · · · · · · ·

My healing is a lifelong journey into greater self-discovery and awareness. I reclaim my personal power, and appreciate my sacred body. I celebrate the power of life that attracts what I need to be whole in body, mind, and spirit. Today, I live my life gracefully receiving the feelings and awakenings of my ever-changing bodymind.

	The Tree of Knowledge	The Tree of Life
The Supreme Agency	The conscious mind through the gaining of knowledge. The intellect can be used to solve every problem or challenge that might ever occur.	Life itself, through a fuller, richer experience of life. Life contains all the miracles and wisdom of the universe, and all solutions to every challenge that might ever occur.
How Success is Achieved	By manipulation of the environment and others. Insulation of the individual from unwanted events, circumstances, and situations is vital.	By being sensitive to the timing and rhythms of nature, as well as the rhythms, pulsations, and vibrations of our body. Every step in life then becomes obvious, and requires little work other than to be awake and aware.
Relationships	Valued for what they can offer us in achieving personal advancement or success.	Valued for expanding our participation in the world; for nurturing, and being nurtured by, the people and opportunities that come into our life.
Physical Symptoms	Viewed as annoyances or interruptions in life, to be eliminated, controlled, or avoided.	Viewed as gifts that have an important message to give us, and that guide us toward healing and a deeper experience of life.
Health	The state in which the individual is not deterred from living a normal life. Achieving our personal goals without physical limitations or discomfort.	The state of optimal physical, emotional, mental, social, and spiritual well-being. Health is associated with gaining a deeper connection with the vibrations, pulsations, and rhythms of life through our bodymind.
Solutions Chosen	Exclusive, competitive, and logical. More is better. The more complicated, the higher the educational degree, the more difficult to master, or the more sacrifice, money, or risk is involved, the greater the dividend or benefit. A greater result requires greater intellect or force.	Inclusive, noncompetitive, and illogical. Those that magically appear or become self evident at the time of need. Internal biological and spiritual forces guide the process, which may not always be logical. Solutions often include unexpected gifts that life presents us.
Avoidance	Avoid the unexpected, chaotic, emotional, or spiritual unless prior planning allows it to be controlled.	Avoid ideas, practices, and situations that do not seem to work in our life, including attitudes and actions that separate us from other people, or our bodymind and its feelings, rhythms, and sensations. Avoid whatever detracts from our experience of wonder and awe for the power of life.

Part 3

. . . .

Biomedical Myths

Centuries ago, evil spirits were widely believed to be the cause of disease. Dressed in ceremonial garb, the medicine men and women of the time would chant, pray, dance, and perform rituals to drive away the offending spirits. This often required that the patient be brought close to death through procedures like burning and bloodletting. At the delicate juncture between life and death, the invading entity would be expected to leave the body. Leeches, roots, herbs, ground-up animal parts, and other medicinal compounds were frequently used in performing this dramatic event.

Toward the end of the nineteenth century, the allopathic physician began to take on the ancient role of ceremonial healer, especially in the United States. Natural healers, particularly those involved in herbal medicine and homeopathy, were gradually replaced by allopathic physicians. The practice of medicine was shifting from an art form, involving the application of natural remedies, into a "science." Instead of people being victimized by evil spirits that destroyed their health, bacteria became the villain. By the 1950s, bacteria lost its status as the evil offender, and viruses became the primary cause of disease. Viruses then became less popular, and faulty DNA was blamed for victimizing people with poor health and disease.

Today, although the methods have changed, the basic myths remain the same. Both the philosophy and practice of modern medicine represent the epitome of cultural surrender to the Tree of Knowledge. Present-day teaching hospitals have become the successors to ancient ritualistic practices, where both humans and laboratory animals have been sacrificed in the name of medical progress. The doctor's intuitive sense of the patient, achieved by listening to the patient's heart, evaluating the pulse, and taking a detailed personal history, has been replaced by an impersonal, mechanistic application of science. The physician of the past customarily made house calls and was well acquainted with both the patient and the patient's entire family. The family doctor understood the family's dynamics, and developed a sense of intimacy with his patients.

Like house calls, listening to the patient's heart is a diagnostic tool that may soon be one of a past era. Use of a stethoscope and palpating for the pulse is not as highly regarded as procedures like ultrasonic testing or electrocardiograms. Nor is either of these procedures as highly revered as those involving a hospital stay and the injection of a toxic dye into the bloodstream. Modern medicine no longer even pretends to "listen to the heart" of the patient. The stethoscopic evaluation of the heart is a dying art form that is no longer a part of the core curricula of most medical schools; it has been replaced by the objectivity of technology.

The physician's intuitive sense of evaluation is being replaced by complex, expensive, and even dangerous testing procedures. Consistent with the old curing myth, if the test fulfills these criteria, the greater the sacrifice the patient has made at the altar of medicine, and the greater the chances of having the God of Medicine observe her plight and act in her favor. With test results in hand, the physician can then condemn the patient with a threatening, or even "terminal," diagnosis. Like the medicine men and women of yesterday, the modern physician can place us in purgatory until further tests are done, or absolve us through an often-dangerous treatment, like surgery, radiation, or chemotherapy.

If we survive the treatment, we often feel as though we have passed through the gates of hell and won a war against the Devil himself. If our condition should improve, it is because of the ritual treatment, and if we succumb to the evil disease, it is because the power of the demon was greater than the power of the God of Medicine. If we are cured, all the physical, emotional, and financial sacrifices involved in treating the evil condition are worth our suffering.

Without question, millions of people have been helped or "saved" by allopathic treatments. The prevailing biomedical myths have led to wonderful discoveries about the pathological process, the mechanical repair of tissues, and the nature and function of different parts of the body. Allopathy has also taught us about the frailties of the human body and its physical and psychological limits. This section on biomedical myths is not meant to criticize allopathic physicians, their intentions, or their methods. Instead, I will be questioning the myths upon which modern medicine is based.

Challenging the Biomedical Myth

Biomedical theory and practice are heavily influenced by and inseparable from our culture. Therefore, in this section we find ourselves face-to-face with many of the same stories that underlie our social myths. According to the prevailing biomedical myths, the human body cannot be trusted. Disease is considered practically inevitable, and degeneration is regarded as natural. Doing something to treat an illness is almost always better than doing nothing at all, even if the vast majority of illness is self-limiting. Within the biomedical culture, the following statements are also assumed or implied to be true:

- Science and medicine will liberate us from our natural inclination to be ill.
- The more money spent on research to study disease or other "evils" affecting the bodymind, the healthier people will be.
- Alternative methods of healing work because of the patient's belief in them, yet allopathic medicine works because it is "scientific."

- People are basically foolish, ignorant, and incapable of making effective choices in life; thus we need an educated physician to help us survive in this hostile world we live in.
- There must be a physical cause for every ailment.
- To understand disease is to understand health.
- Health is the absence of symptoms, pain, and abnormal laboratory tests.
- Pregnancy, childbirth, and aging are medical conditions.
- The highest level of health for a patient involves never being disturbed by any symptom or condition of the body that he does not like.
- Health is achieved by declaring war on the aberrant parts.
- External factors that promote disease need to be controlled or eliminated.

Some prevailing views of modern medicine were recently questioned by Bernard Lown, M.D., Chairman of the Lown Cardiovascular Research Foundation, and Thomas B. Graboys, M.D., Associate Clinical Professor of Medicine at Harvard Medical School. In a letter published in *The New Yorker*, they wrote:

> We believe that the modern medical model has become increasingly reductionist: human beings are seen as repositories of malfunctioning organs that need repair. This view results in an onslaught of tests and assaultive procedures that purport to give definite answers in a

field fraught with uncertainty. Doctors often take refuge behind technology because it is easier and less time-consuming than talking with a complex human being who is their patient.[1]

According to the *Journal of the American Medical Association*, the current leading causes of death in the United States are, in order: heart disease, cancer, stroke, and adverse drug reactions. Since nearly one out of every four hospital admissions have been reported to be the result of adverse drug reactions, there is no way of knowing the number of people whose deaths, thought to be caused by disease, may instead have been caused by adverse reactions to a prescribed medication. The same article reported that 180,000 people die each year in American hospitals due to incorrectly prescribed medicines.[2] This figure is currently greater than all crimes and accidents combined.

In spite of billions of dollars spent on cancer research, the incidence of this disease, with all of the expensive, dangerous, and lethal treatments, is higher than ever. Studies have shown that the consumption of meat and animal fats poses a strong risk factor in heart disease and cancer, yet many fast-food restaurants are serving larger hamburgers than ever. Hospitals routinely serve patients suffering from heart disease meat, butter, and milk. Patients with cancer are given gelatin loaded with artificial colors, flavors, and sweeteners that are known to be carcinogenic to laboratory animals.

With all the recent advances in medical treatment, heart attacks, which were a rarity a hundred years ago, are a leading cause of death today. Recent clinical and laboratory studies have seriously questioned the validity of the theory that a blocked coronary artery is the primary cause of a heart attack. The angiogram, an invasive test to evaluate coronary artery blockages, poses significant risks, and has often been discredited. In many cases, bypass surgery is considered unnecessary and dangerous.

Some of the most commonly prescribed anti-hypertensive medications to control high blood pressure are often considered ineffective, and may actually produce an increased risk of heart attack and stroke. A medical study of 291 patients concluded that calcium channel blockers used as anti-hypertensive agents appeared to increase the risk of heart attack, even in otherwise "healthy" hypertensive patients. A compilation of sixteen prior studies had shown that, compared to a placebo, several calcium channel blockers actually tripled a patient's risk of death.[3] An estimated six million Americans take calcium blockers, spending about $3.5 billion on the drugs each year. This is in spite of the data demonstrating that diet, exercise, and meditation significantly assist the body in eliminating not only hypertension, but advanced heart disease as well.

In the United States, flu deaths among adults continue to rise in spite of massive flu inoculation programs. Results of a clinical study presented at the American Geriatrics Society in Atlanta in 1997 suggested that people over sixty-five may not benefit from annual flu shots. According to Dr. Haim Dannengerg of the Hadassah University Hospital in Jerusalem, the study showed that the subjects (whose average age was seventy-two) who had been given repeated flu vaccines had lower antibody levels against three major strains of flu than those who were not vaccinated. Dr. Dannengerg also found, "Our study showed that a decreased immune response to some influenza strains may follow repeated annual vaccinations."[4]

Antibiotics, once considered allopathic medicine's answer to infectious disease, are being viewed as the cause of dangerous super-infections. The use of antibiotics to fight three common respiratory conditions — colds, upper respiratory tract infections, and bronchitis — is now considered ineffective at best. Seventy percent of all infants in the United States are subjected to their first course of antibiotics during the first two hundred days of life.[5] Middle ear infections are the most common reason, despite the fact that amoxicillin, the most commonly prescribed antibiotic, was demonstrated to be ineffective for this purpose in most cases. Many physicians still prescribe antibiotics for these illnesses despite evidence that they do little or nothing to treat the problems.

An editorial published in the *Journal of the American Medical Association* stated: "Unrealistic patient expectations coupled with insufficient time to discuss with patients why an antibiotic is not needed" are the major reasons why physicians over prescribe antibiotic drugs when they know the drugs will be ineffective and make the patients prone to superinfections.[6] The gospel of modern medicine that inflated the importance of prescription drugs and surgery in the restoration and maintenance of health is beginning to change, but the change will not be easy. The physician, who is the quasi-ecclesiastic representative of the old story, must now communicate a new story with the "congregation," or patients. Communicating a change in the old myth by telling patients that such drugs may not be necessary is not an easy task without referring to (and questioning) the underlying mythology itself. The doctor must not only accept the changing roles between doctor and patient, and treatment and healing, but also assume a greater role as storyteller.

At the core of the biomedical approach to curing is fear. Delaying or refusing treatment within the medical mythos can be likened to not accepting the edict of a high priest or not taking the sacrament of the Church a few hundred years ago. Fear motivates us to adhere to the story that preaches hope for the individual only through the sanctioned rituals of the dominant medical culture. Healing modalities with a different story that don't follow the exact procedures of the dominant "church of medicine" are attacked and dismissed without objective evaluation. Excommunication is never pleasant. As we have seen in cases where individuals challenge cultural mythologies, punishment may be severe for those who are not "of the faith" or who convert to other beliefs regarding the philosophy of health and healing.

Those who question popular applications of the allopathic model are often met with bigotry, ignorance, and attack. Parents who reject the medical story, and refuse what they consider potentially dangerous vaccinations or medical treatment for their children, are subject to ridicule and even criminal prosecution as child abusers. A doctor who fails to recommend the treatment of choice for a serious disease, regardless of its safety or effectiveness, can lose her license, face heavy fines, and even risk a jail sentence.

Even when evidence is published in respected medical journals documenting the dangers of certain drugs and procedures, the unquestioned and almost religious belief in the biomedical model still rules the decision-making process among doctors and patients alike. If the above findings applied to practitioners of any other healing art, including chiropractors, acupuncturists, or herbalists, their professions would have been eliminated, their proponents ridiculed or thrown in jail, and their schools closed by order of the courts. Instead, the medical establishment today enjoys incredible prestige. Philanthropists donate billions of dollars for medical research, construction of hospitals, and other curing establishments. Even when it is proven that certain drugs or procedures never worked or no longer work, new treatments, based on the old biomedical story, are generated every day.

Other than advancements in repair or trauma surgery (which are amazing in their ability to save lives and restore the quality of life), conventional medicine in America probably kills more people each year through its procedures, treatments, and story than almost any other cause. The majority of people who read this will still resort to the same medical institutions for care; others will question the system. I suggest, instead, that we question the underlying myths that generate and empower the prevailing medical culture. I contend that unless we evaluate the myths that control our lives, we will often seek the same choices we have been trained to choose, even if these choices are killing us.

A New Story

Currently, a grassroots revolution is taking place, with both patients and physicians demanding greater flexibility within the medical system. Procedures that have long been viewed as miracles of modern medicine are losing their status, not only within the academic community, but also within the "home court" of organized medicine itself. A growing number of well-intentioned practitioners are attempting to change the prevailing system by adding alternative treatments to the repertoire of existing practices. Little of substance can be done, however, without changing the fundamental stories or myths.

In the old story, we are a victim of a condition we do not want, and we approach the problem from this perspective. It is not a question of what procedures are most effective, or what therapy is most useful to treat a particular disease or condition. Whether we use drugs, herbs, nutritional supplements, acupuncture, homeopathy, or any other therapy to treat a disease, the basic story remains the same: We are attempting to *eliminate the condition* by treating or *curing* it. Rather than considering the hypertension, asthma, cancer, heart disease, or emotional disorder as "things" that need fixing, we need a different approach.

We must dispel the myths of the past that empower the institution of medicine, and spawn not only the same kind of thoughts and discoveries as the old model, but subsequently limit its evolution. We need to create a whole new story that empowers the individual, and describes the healing magic that can occur. Instead of placing an overemphasis on treatment, the new story will ask us to look at the relationships between people and events, seek a greater trust in the body's capacity to heal, and inspire hope within the patient.

Although the current story can exist within the new one, the old mythology can no longer dominate the way we view disease, health, and life itself. It must move to a stage of deeper understanding and compassion for patients. The new story will view the individual's role in disease as being at least as important as external factors. Emotional, spiritual, and mental influences will be given at least equal footing with chemical, mechanical, and physical factors.

The new story will not attack disease or symptoms as evil invaders that hold a patient hostage, requiring a medical SWAT team to "take them out." It will allow for medical intervention in cases of trauma, while focusing on the body's innate striving for its own sense of organization and healing. Instead of attempting to make the patient healthier, it will help us to understand and experience attributes of a healthy bodymind and a healthy life. While the new story will allow for symptoms and even disease to exist without intervention at times, it will also provide a learning process that helps us to reorient our lives. It is one that will call, whenever possible, for the most conservative approach first.

The new story will assist us in the healing process. Even when surgical intervention is performed, the new healing model will support our own self-healing strategy, and rely on the body's innate intelligence to heal. The kind of life choices we make will be part of an overall health assessment, involving factors like the type of food we eat, freedom from an electromagnetic environment, and interpersonal strategies that support love, trust, respect, and self-reliance.

Finally, the way the doctor speaks to us about our condition and healing will change. In the new story, the "medical clergy" will relinquish their role as authority figures who know everything. Physicians will instead serve as trusted role models with reverence for life and compassion for both the individual and the human community at large.

· 11 ·

healing myth

Every disease or illness can be traced to a physical cause.

"Doctor, when you see the X-rays, will you know what caused the pain?" "Will the lab test tell us what is making me sick?"

If a diagnostic tool reveals a blocked coronary artery, calcified spinal joints, high blood pressure, or high cholesterol, does this tell us why we feel ill, or indicate a true prognosis? Could a test result appear "normal" when we are feeling so bad? If our quality of life was not impaired, and if we had a sense of well-being, would we really care about these physical findings? How does the way we live our life impact the physical findings? Will a change in our life influence our health and well-being?

The myth that "every disease can be traced to a physical cause" is part of a cultural hallucination that began years ago. In the seventeenth century, René Descartes, a French philosopher and mathematician, advanced the idea that anything objective, material, and measurable belonged to science, while the subjective, spiritual, and immeasurable belonged to the realm of religion and the Church. His ideas were further advanced by philosophers who taught that anything pertaining to the human mind should be relegated to the field of psychology. Philosophical concepts relating to the body, mind, and spirit were divided into separate "camps," as proponents of each had their own view on the primacy of their story.

The study of medicine as strictly a physical science seemed to work rather well until the following discoveries were made: Physical matter, which was thought to be made of small particles, or atoms, was determined to be mostly empty space. The atom was discovered to have smaller subunits, of almost no mass, that possess an electrical charge and travel in distinct paths around the nucleus. Then it was discovered that, at different points in time, the electron was found at every point in the universe, with a *probability* of being in a path around the nucleus. Other atomic subunits, such as the positron, were later discovered and postulated to be capable of moving backward in time. It was found that the smallest particles of the atom were all interchangeable, and that these "packages of energy" and "packages of matter" were also interchangeable. Yet another discovery was that atomic particles sometimes functioned as waves, or nonparticles. The nature of matter wasn't as simple as it was originally believed.

The Emotional Factor

More recently, scientists suggest that with every emotion we experience, certain tissues, including nerve cells and circulating white blood cells, vibrate at the particular frequency associated with a chemical (or peptide) attaching to the surface of the cell. Candace Pert, Ph.D., the noted biochemist and author of *Molecules of Emotion: Why You Feel the Way You Feel*, says, "We can no longer think of emotions as having less validity than physical, material substance, but instead must see them as cellular signals that are involved in the process of translating information into physical reality, literally transforming mind into matter. Emotions are at the nexus between mind and matter, going back and forth between the two and influencing both."

It may be said that the tone of the cell membrane, its biochemical interactions with neuropeptides, and its energy circulation and vibration *are* the emotion. Thus, the physical and emotional are aspects of the same process. Likewise, what is called "spiritual" is at least partly an awareness of subtle energy in the body associated with certain peptides being activated in the brain.

Although diet is an important part of healthy living, many times it is not so much "what you eat" as "what's eating you" that may promote heart disease. Factors such as tension, frustration, and sadness are known to double the risk of heart attacks, and even cause permanent heart damage.

The Social Factor

Roseto and Bangor are neighboring cities in Pennsylvania. Roseto was the subject of a thirty-year study undertaken by Dr. Benjamin Falcone, a physician in Roseto, who reported that statistics in his city defied all the usual predictors of heart attack. The city's population of 1,600 was almost entirely composed of a large closely knit Italian community, and reported less than one half the rate of death from heart attack than Bangor, a more culturally diverse community of about 5,000 inhabitants. These low rates were found despite the fact that both communities shared similar levels of cardiac-related risk factors, like smoking, drinking, and diet. Although those with cholesterol over 200 are considered to have twice the risk of heart attack, less than 20 percent of those in Roseto who had cholesterol level of 200 or higher suffered a heart attack, while the statistics for Bangor were similar to the United States as a whole.

Dr. Falcone determined that what set Roseto apart from Bangor was that its residents enjoyed much closer family ties and greater community cohesion. During the time of the study, the rate of heart attacks rose in Bangor as family ties broke town, while that in Roseto remained stable. This study demonstrated that human biology is significantly influenced by social environment.

Studies have shown that a person with fewer social interactions had four times the risk of contracting the common cold than average, while those enjoying frequent social interactions had reduced chances of developing a cold. This evidence would appear to conflict with the expected outcome that the people with more social contacts would also have an increased exposure to the cold virus. If we consider the person first and the organism second, the individual who has more social contact with others may have activated an aspect of the immune system that promotes a healthier internal state and greater resistance to breakdown and infection.

The Relationship, Timing, and Other Contributing Factors

While the sciences and philosophies developed over the past millennium effectively built distinct and comprehensive areas of study, they also separated the inherent interconnectedness of the various disciplines and the stories we use to describe our physical, emotional, mental, and spiritual realities. The storytellers of each discipline encourage us to adhere to the status quo, and discourage us from embracing a new story to describe our bodymind and our relationship with the world around us.

Symptom and disease care (the basis of Western medicine), exist on one continuum, while illness and wellness (which include the experience of our self, our body, and our life) exist on another. Physical, emotional, and mental states are interdependent and inseparable. When the physical body alone is evaluated as a basis of health or disease, the influences of the other factors are ignored, and an incomplete picture is drawn.

The practice of mainstream medicine is "part centered," while the focus of healing is "relationship centered." Understanding a single part does not tell us about the relationships between various parts. Just as a group of athletic superstars does not necessarily make a winning team, a team composed of average athletes does not necessarily make a losing one. The relationship and timing of the interaction of the parts can be more important than the parts themselves. That is why there is no such thing as a single cause and effect. To assume that such a cause-and-effect dynamic exists, we have to discount the stress, tensions, and patterns of information *already in place* when a particular event occurs.

The timing of an event or situation can have a tremendous effect on us. Someone may make an insulting comment to us on a particular day, and we may disregard the statement with no impact on our outlook or our physiology. If we hear the same comment on another day, it may cause us to be upset for hours or days, or even trigger an asthmatic episode, sciatic pain, or a heart attack. This is because chemical stresses within our system, whether due to alcohol, cigarettes, medications, or other factors in our life, will also influence our response.

Let's consider a woman named Mary who has a "bad" cold. She is sneezing, coughing, and has a headache and a fever. She is in bed for two days, and then is able to resume work. Jill, her sister, comes down with a runny nose shortly after Mary's symptoms appear, but is otherwise unaffected. Jill's husband, Scott, is hospitalized for two weeks with pneumonia, while Mandy, their daughter, is unaffected. Meanwhile, Mandy's best friend, Dawn, develops a sinus condition that lasts for three months.

Is the "bug" the cause of their symptoms and ill health, or is the relative health or well-being of their bodymind the primary factor? Louis Pasteur, the French biochemist and bacteriologist who developed the germ theory, is reported to have said, "The microbe is nothing; the soil is everything." By "the soil," he meant the body, as it is the body that harbors the germs and then becomes sick. There are many contributing factors in the loss of health and the development of illness. And there are many contributing factors in the restoration of health and the process of healing.

Often when an individual has a physical symptom that is resistant to treatment, the physical problem is not the real situation that needs attention. If a physical trauma has occurred, the question to be asked is: "What else was happening in your life when the accident occurred?" In his book *Travels*, Michael Crichton refers to the experiences of a Swiss physician who had taken up a post in the Alps during the 1930s. As both an avid skier, and a doctor who often treated ski injuries, he was curious about the cause of skiing accidents. Crichton wrote, "He asked his patients why they had their accidents, expecting to hear that they had taken a turn too quickly, or hit a patch of rock or some other skiing explanation. To his surprise, everyone gave a psychological reason for the accident. They were upset about something, they were distracted, and so on."

People do not attract physical and emotional traumas separately. In our culture, however, the physical expression is considered "real" and approachable, while emotional or psychological factors are rarely considered. What is often blamed as the cause for our loss of health, is at best merely associated with it, rather than the cause of it. As mentioned earlier, once our focus is on the physical cause, we can avoid responsibility for the events that led to the crisis, and that kept us from correcting or arresting it to begin with.

In healing, it is important to remember that we are more than a physical body; we are energy in motion, as well as vibration, pulsation, and rhythm. The energy that comprises the bodymind is intimately connected to the wealth of energy and information in the Universe.

. . . . *HEALING MAGIC* . . . .

I surrender blaming a single cause for my symptoms, pain, or lack of health. I acknowledge all aspects of my life that may have inhibited or altered the expression of life energy within me. My symptoms and pain remind me of my need to participate more fully in the world. I celebrate and bless the free exchange of energy and information within my bodymind.

· 12 ·

healing myth

Symptoms and disease are inconvenient "obstacles"
that need to be controlled or eliminated.

Imagine a narrow road with hairpin turns hugging the edge of a mountain. Every year, dozens of cars fall off the mountain, crashing into the valley below. One approach to the problem would be to post warning signs ahead of the dangerous turns, reduce the speed limit, and erect guardrails to prevent cars from going off the road. A second approach to the problem might be to build larger emergency and operating rooms at the local hospital to better accommodate the dead and injured passengers. We could also build more auto body shops and staff them with highly trained mechanics to fix the smashed cars.

The latter approach is much like the old biomedical story. In the old myth, symptoms of disease are inconvenient messages of the body that need to be eliminated in order to continue on the same road we have always been on. The injured passengers and smashed cars at the bottom of the valley are seen as the problem that needs to be "fixed."

In the new story, symptoms are seen as warning signs, telling us that if we continue down the same road, there is danger ahead. Disease symptoms are not mistakes; they come from the innate wisdom of the bodymind. Symptoms are the means by which the wisdom of our body attempts to modify our behavior, increase its ability to experience energy, dissipate energy, move freely, and relieve tension. The bodymind wants to tell us its story, express its needs, and let us know what it's feeling. By becoming aware of, and responding to, these inner messages, there is the promise that our symptoms and condition may easily be resolved.

Charlie's Story

Joe was a borderline student in high school. He was mechanically inclined, and liked to tinker with old cars. His dad drank heavily and would beat both Joe and his mother. At times, Joe would come to school with black-and-blue marks on his arms and legs, claiming that he got banged up at sports. He stayed late at school or hung around the auto repair shop in town, avoiding his home as much as possible.

During Joe's senior year in high school, he met Christine, who was a junior at the same school. They soon found something they shared in common: Christine's mother drank and her father traveled a lot, making the home environment less than pleasant.

One day Christine discovered that she was pregnant, and the couple decided to do the "right thing" and get married. They had no money and their parents had no extra funds to lend them, so Joe dropped out of school and began to work long hours as a mechanic. Joe did not want this child; he knew that being a father would require more work, more money, and more responsibility. "This kid is going to take my best years away from me," he protested. Arguing and fighting became the predominant pattern of relating to each other. Christine did not want the baby either, but decided to make the best of her situation. As she got closer to full term, Joe began drinking, and Christine increased her cigarette consumption. Because Christine did not want to get fat, her diet consisted primarily of low-fat packaged foods and diet soda.

When the baby was due, they checked into the local hospital, where Christine was "prepped," given an enema, and confined to bed. An IV was inserted into her arm and a fetal monitor placed on her abdomen. Because her contractions were painful, painkillers were added to the IV drip, thus drugging the baby through the mother's bloodstream. Christine's contractions were slow, so doctors gave her another drug to hasten labor. Her contractions, rather than being timed by natural rhythms between the mother and child, were now placed on turbo boost with little regard for the relationship between Christine and her baby. Christine was given an epidural anesthetic to help relieve pain, and was ordered to remain on her back through delivery, a typical process for millions of births. On her back, with her legs strapped in leather and spread apart, the blood supply to the uterus was reduced at a time when it had to do the most work. Christine was on her back despite her desire to move, squat, and change positions.

The doctor then "assisted" the baby in birth. The baby was pulled from the womb by the neck, inflicting more force to his neck and spine than an adult would experience if involved in a major automobile accident. After birth, the baby was slapped. This practice is often necessary when a newborn is drugged. Pain may have to be inflicted to remind the baby forcibly to take its first breath. Burning silver nitrate was placed into the child's eyes just in case Christine had venereal disease. It was so painful that he could not open his eyes for two days. Born into a cold room and twice pricked on the foot to draw blood, he was taken from his mother and weighed on a cold scale.

Little Charlie, as he was named, was then wrapped in a blanket and placed in a plastic pen to be given formula on schedule, irrespective of his body's needs. Since epidural anesthesia is often associated with fever, Charlie and mother were treated with antibiotics and kept in the hospital for several days. The infant was without his mother's energy, affection, and love, which are natural and vital to a newborn. During the first days of his life, Charlie had learned that breathing can be difficult, holding the breath is natural, and the skin is a place for pain.

Charlie came home and cried. He was placed in a separate room to "cry it out" because his parents were warned not to allow their baby to "manipulate" them with his demands. The baby was fed formula according to a strict schedule, and was given more antibiotics.

Mom and Dad began fighting more often, and Charlie was seen as both the cause and the focus of their problems. Several months after birth, Charlie was inoculated against several childhood diseases, and developed asthma soon thereafter. Although the asthma medication helped him to breathe, he often became irritable and hyperactive. After Charlie entered grade school, he was diagnosed with an attention deficit disorder, and was given another drug to control this condition.

Even though he was still a young child, Charlie learned some important lessons. In addition to learning that the skin is a place to feel discomfort, and that separation from loved ones and their affectionate touch is natural, he learned that it is normal to be sick and natural to take drugs to get through life. Finally, he learned that he is a victim of circumstances he could never control.

While taking physical education in middle school, Charlie experienced further insults to his spine and body in soccer and football. He never complained, because he learned that if he expressed discomfort or pain, the cheerleaders would no longer shout his name. He learned to stifle his body's cues and signals, and to repress what he did not like to feel.

As his father had done years before, Charlie got his high school sweetheart pregnant. This presented the opportunity to get out of his house, where his parents were often hostile and abusive. He quit school, got a job, and moved in with his girlfriend. Their relationship was not unlike that of Charlie's parents years ago, and was characterized by alcohol, arguments, and abusive behavior. A heavy smoker, Charlie's high blood pressure was kept under control by medication. Charlie thought he was healthy, and his doctor confirmed it, but one day he picked up a heavy box, and fell on the floor in pain.

What was the cause of Charlie's symptoms? Did he injure a disc, or suffer a sudden heart attack? Was the chest pain and shortness of breath due to lung cancer? Did cancer develop because of Charlie's heavy smoking, or was the heavy smoking due to other factors that might contribute to cancer? Charlie's symptoms can be viewed in many ways, but is the heart attack, or cancer, or other disease, the *cause* of his ill health or a *manifestation* of it?

This is not unlike the story of a person falling off a tall building. On the way down, he repeats, "So far so good, so far so good!" When he suddenly lands on the pavement below, is the fall responsible for his fatal situation, or is it the multitude of factors that led to it instead? If a man suddenly drops dead of a heart attack, or is told he has late-stage cancer, his family is often shocked and exclaims that he was "never sick a day in his life." Yet we can see from Charlie's story that many factors could have contributed to his illness.

The living systems of the body must exchange information and energy and work together harmoniously to create wholeness and health. Studying Charlie's diseased heart, lungs, or spinal disc will not tell us how the body maintains its systems in good health. It may only tell us the "path of logic" or "pathology" of that part of the body whose structure or function was modified due to interruptions in the flow of information and energy.

Symptoms of illness, and illness itself, are the bodymind's attempt to more effectively express the energy that is blocked or unable to circulate. The movement, effective use, and dissipation of energy are primary in life. Once again, disease is not a mistake of a stupid body; it is the body's attempt to reorganize its energy systems to allow for a greater exchange of information and energy and thus a greater expression of consciousness.

. . . . *HEALING MAGIC* . . . .

My symptoms alert me that my bodymind needs more self-respect, compassion, and my focused attention. They may require that I spend quality time with myself, or even guide me to change my direction and choices in life. I patiently accept my symptoms as information, vibration, and pulsation, with a story to tell me about my life's journey.

· 13 ·

healing myth

*Healing means symptoms and disease disappear
or come under control.*

In healing, our symptoms and disease may or may not disappear or come under control, yet often we will gain greater insight into our life, and learn to be more compassionate toward ourselves and others. The healing process involves a progressive expression of more of our being. Healing brings us to a greater awareness of all parts of our bodymind, along with their experiences, stories, and energies. Although we may still, for the time being, have various symptoms or ailments, we can be more alive, more aware, more creative, and at peace.

Eddy's Story

Eddy was a powerfully built man in his late thirties who had come to my office for help with his hip. He began chiropractic care because his wife felt that a release of tension in his spine might reduce the pain in his hip. She also hoped that if her husband were pain-free, he might be easier to get along with.

Eddy didn't want to be in my office, or in the office of any practitioner. In fact, whenever I saw him, he was miserable in every conceivable way. While in the reception area, every remark out of his mouth was either insulting, nasty, or depressing. Many families would visit our office, including children and even their pets. The cats hissed at Eddy, the dogs growled, and mothers asked their children not to go near him. When Eddy was in the adjusting room, any levity that existed would soon be replaced by a dark cloud of depression. It got so bad that patients would not arrive until Eddy had left for home. After each visit, he rubbed his hand on his left hip and repeated the same line: "Nope, it still hurts here."

After a few weeks of care, Eddy began to lighten up. He stopped complaining about everything. Children and even some animals approached him in the waiting room. He actually began to tell jokes while waiting his turn to see me. Clinically, I noticed significant changes in Eddy's spinal mobility, body symmetry, and muscle tension patterns. He was expressing a slow, deep respiration that gently rocked his spine. This, in turn, enhanced the circulation of oxygen and nutrients, and promoted greater ease in his body. During each visit, I told him about the positive changes I was observing in his spine and mood, yet his response remained predictable: "Nope, Doc, it still hurts here," as he pointed to his left hip.

I was frustrated when Eddy did not acknowledge his progress, but how could I communicate that healing meant more than his pain going away? I spoke to a colleague about this dilemma, and he suggested that I ask members of Eddy's family about the changes they had seen in Eddy's life since he began seeing me.

A few days later, Eddy brought his son Tommy into the office to get adjusted. I thought to myself, "Here is my chance!" I asked Tommy, who was about ten years old, "What do you like best about Daddy since he started coming to see me?" Little Tommy looked somewhat uncomfortable, and squirmed a bit. After a short pause he slowly replied, "Oh, he stopped hitting me, and quit punching Mommy in the face." Upon hearing this, Eddy drew his son to him as tears flowed from his eyes. Here was a man who prided himself on the fact that he never cried. Eddy once bragged that he did not even cry when his father died. I felt as though something magical had transformed the office. Eddy's hip pain had not been resolved, but aspects of his relationship between himself and his wife, his son, his friends and co-workers had changed. Eddy was healing.

At this point, I made an important decision: I would never again judge a patient's healing by the presence or absence of a particular symptom. After all, what could make a greater difference in Eddy's life than that of a happier, more harmonious relationship with family, friends, and the world around him? Each of us needs healing throughout our lifetime, regardless of the treatment we receive or the resolution of our symptoms, pain, or problems.

Jamie's Story

Jamie was an active woman of fifty who smoked two packs of cigarettes a day. Every winter of her adult life, she had experienced a severe bout of pneumonia. As a prelude to pneumonia, Jamie developed chest pain, congestion, fluid buildup, and a fever. Beginning in January, she would be bedridden for about six weeks, and occasionally hospitalized. Her curing routine was predictable: antibiotics, cough suppressants, bed rest, and her mother's chicken noodle soup.

After being in my care for a few months, January arrived, and although the same symptoms arose once more, something was different this time. Rather than feeling like a victim of her condition, Jamie told me that she welcomed her illness as an opportunity to resolve something she had previously been unable to resolve. When asked what she was talking about specifically, she replied that she didn't know yet.

Jamie's attitude about herself and her circumstance was certainly different: that year she decided — without any prompting by me or my staff — not to take any medication for as long as possible. When she became sick, her pneumonia was no longer "under control," and her fever went higher than ever before (104 degrees F). Although Jamie's chest still hurt more than ever when she coughed, she was in bed for only two and a half weeks instead of the customary six weeks.

When she returned to my office, Jamie shared her excitement over having quit smoking. She had began to clear self-destructive patterns from her life. Jamie was experiencing trust, gratitude, and respect for herself, as well as for her body and its wisdom. Though it appeared that Jamie was experiencing the same pneumonia she had had for the previous twenty-six years, Jamie was healing.

. . . . *HEALING MAGIC* . . . .

I accept myself unconditionally, with all my symptoms, conditions, and glorious imperfections. I am healing in spite of the imperfections that still appear in my body and my life. The healing power of my bodymind is more powerful than I ever imagined. As I heal, I experience my whole self, including my light and my shadows.

· 14 ·

healing myth

If symptoms disappear shortly after treatment,
the treatment is responsible.

The myth that treating our symptoms is the cause for us regaining our health is based on the belief that only outside forces cause symptoms or disease to take place within us. We are the victims of illness, and events or circumstances *outside* ourselves are to blame for our loss of health.

In the mechanistic model of healing, all causes or cures of health or disease fall into neat packages that we generally do not question. This model teaches that disease is the result of specific causes and effects. It does not consider multiple contributing factors, or a person's susceptibility to a particular disease. For example, it has long been assumed that a good diet and regular exercise contribute to a healthy heart, while a poor diet and lack of exercise contribute to heart disease. Yet, an article appearing in the *Journal of the American*

Medical Association stated that tension, frustration, and sadness double the risk of a heart attack and permanent heart damage.

Cause-and-effect analysis may be suitable in the chemistry or pharmacology lab, but it fails miserably in the laboratory called life. Imagine a sculptor who strikes a piece of marble with a thousand blows. With one final blow, the marble cracks and the sculpture is destroyed. Was it the final blow that cracked the stone, or did it merely contribute to a succession of blows that caused the crack? Was there a crack in the stone when the sculptor began? Did the sculptor lack the proper skill? Was the position of his hammer the cause? Perhaps the blame can be placed on the person who selected the marble, or the people who transported it to the sculptor's studio.

It is time to question the habit of blaming a single variable, or the last action taken before a symptom appears, for the cause of our illness. It is time to move past the mechanistic view of simple cause and effect and embrace the concept of open, interactive systems. The current perspective on healing looks for an immediate answer to gratify our desire to know the cause of our illness. Whenever we judge a situation and attribute a single cause to it, we ignore the complex interrelationship of people, events, and circumstances, and the energy circulating within us. If we recognize the myriad of interrelated factors that contribute to our health or to our loss of health, our physiology is not primed to condemn and attack ourselves or others. Many contributing factors are indirect, and therefore, delayed. In fact, in health and disease, indirect factors may be more important than direct ones.

Robert's Story

Robert was an attorney who disliked his work. He once said to me, "Who likes lawyers? I don't." The more he worked, the more helpless he felt. Then Robert developed severe asthma, and his asthma medication appeared to be related to his migraine headaches. The migraine headaches forced him to rest, and resting, in turn, reduced his stress level. As a result, Robert felt less despair about his job. He decided to consult both traditional and alternative health practitioners for his ailments, and this led him to change his diet, begin an exercise program, and learn how to meditate.

After a while, Robert discovered that trying to do something to fix his symptoms was a distraction from dealing with the core issues in his life. He stopped trying to do anything to help himself, and took time off from work because "I just can't breathe, and my head hurts too much to work."

Robert's way of dealing with his symptoms was unique indeed. Whenever he had trouble breathing, he would clutch at his chest and shout, "I can't breathe!" When his head hurt, he moaned, "My head hurts so much, and I hate my work." He would actually place his hands on his head, letting his hands instinctively rub his face and skull with a rhythm of their own.

While at home, he was often bored, so he took up painting while sitting in his den moaning, groaning, and feeling sorry for himself. Then Robert noticed that while painting a picture, his headaches would disappear and he didn't have any difficulty breathing. He produced several beautiful paintings and was proud of them. By the end of one month, Robert felt inspired, fulfilled, and productive. He no longer had trouble breathing, and whenever his head hurt, he closed his eyes and moved the way his body wanted him to move. He told me, "Could you imagine me in a courtroom, or at a real estate closing, running my hands across my body, breathing deeply, and making guttural sounds? It's silly how long I've resisted acting this way. Even more ridiculous is that, until recently, I would never have considered doing this privately at home."

Robert developed a plan to retire from law and devote himself to painting full-time. I don't know whether he did, although I heard that his paintings were on exhibit at a small gallery in a seaside community in California. Work-related stress may have been a cause of Robert's asthma, and the asthma medication may have been the cause of the migraine headaches. The asthma and headaches may have caused Robert to leave work and begin painting. The painting might have been the cause for starting his new life. Robert's story reveals how our symptoms and crises are often inseparable from the many causes and effects that exist in our lives. Instead of attributing causation to any single factor in life, we can see that we are always influenced by a multitude of factors. Nothing works on us or within us alone. This includes those things that we think are causing our problems, and those that seem to be solving them.

. . . . *HEALING MAGIC* . . . .

My symptoms and distress guide me to heal. What worked for me at one point may no longer serve me today. What seemed to hurt me yesterday may be my current remedy. I honor my healing cycles and my participation in a greater plan. The power within me is part of a greater power. I am amazed at how it heals me, in spite of what I consider to be the cause or the cure.

· 15 ·

healing myth

Healing means feeling better.

Healing does not always mean that we will feel better. We cannot heal what we cannot feel, and healing often requires us to feel things we don't like feeling. If we believe the myth that "healing means feeling better," then feeling better becomes our objective instead of simply feeling what our bodymind must feel in order to heal.

The consequences of accepting this myth are twofold: First, it forces us to suppress, combat, or alleviate any circumstance, situation, or awareness that alters the way we are accustomed to living our life. Taking a painkiller or antidepressant may offer temporary relief that lets us carry on as we did before without being aware of, or responsive to, the needs of our bodymind. The benefits derived from our actions may, at best, provide temporary relief from the knowledge that we are not expressing the life we are capable of living. To heal our body and our mind, and to express more of our spirit, our bodymind must first become aware that something needs to be remedied. Once our biology becomes aware of the need, life naturally brings the appropriate elements into play, and provides the "medicine" necessary to heal us.

Second, the myth that "healing means feeling better" compels us to distract ourselves with food, sex, and television, or to become addicted to drugs, gambling, spectator sports, and "retail therapy" at shopping malls. By avoiding our innermost thoughts and feelings, we ignore our bodymind's physical signals, and become even less aware of what we are feeling. After we engage in our typical avoidance strategy, we still feel empty or have more pain and discomfort than we did before.

In the short term, distracting ourselves may feel better than making corrective changes in our life. But once life itself becomes aware of what needs healing, we can finally make the changes that support it. Healing will require us to involve all parts of our being. This includes those parts of us we like, those we don't like, those we remember, those we forgot about, aspects of our life that bring us pain, and those that bring us ecstasy. Bringing the diverse, and often divergent, aspects of our life together is necessary before life can discard what we no longer need. For a short time, we may feel uncomfortable, but over time, healing enables us to better express our spirit, and to feel truly empowered and alive.

Arnold's Story

Arnold had experienced intermittent chest pain for a couple of years. He was in his forties, was thirty pounds overweight, and was considered an overachiever at work. His cardiologist told him that he had a heart valve problem, and he was offered a number of treatment options, including drugs and surgery.

One day as he lay in bed, the pressure in his chest increased. Feeling both angry and fearful, Arnold instinctively rubbed his chest, and at the same time, began to sob. Arnold had never done this before. While he sobbed, the pain spread from his chest to his arms, shoulders, head, and face. His hands became numb. Arnold felt as though he had entered an "altered realm of consciousness" between dreaming and wakefulness. Then, just as he felt he was going to die, he screamed. His scream was filled with grief and sorrow, and he realized he was crying for those deceased family members for whom he had never grieved. This process lasted about six hours.

The following morning, though still sad, Arnold awakened feeling refreshed. He later observed that it was a good thing his wife was not home because she would have called an ambulance to take him to the hospital, where they would have seen his "awakening" as a sign of disease, and tried to arrest it. Years later, Arnold mentioned that the chest discomfort had never returned. In Arnold's case, healing did not necessarily mean feeling better, but rather *better feeling* what he needed to feel.

. . . . *HEALING MAGIC* . . . .

I celebrate the totality of my feelings. I celebrate the individual parts of me, and the individual feelings of those parts. I pay attention to my feelings, knowing that their meaning will become self-evident at the perfect time, in the most exquisite way. I celebrate the healing that occurs in a continuous cycle of pleasure, pain, comfort, and discomfort.

· 16 ·

healing myth

A person may be too far gone to heal.

Medical literature is replete with case histories of individuals who have spontaneously recovered from virtually every type of hopeless situation, including heart disease, cancer, and AIDS. Those who have healed commonly report a change in their priorities and perspectives on life. They find themselves reaching for and affirming a purpose in life that is greater than the normal administration of their daily lives. This shift in consciousness seems to be inspired by the power of life itself, or that field of primary intelligence from which all things are created and to which all things return.

In order for someone to make this shift, some level of healing in the bodymind must already have occurred. Since we cannot resolve a situation from the same consciousness that created it, we must experience a shift in our consciousness before our behavior will change. I have known patients who were aware that their condition would probably not improve, as there appeared to be no "cure" for it. These individuals often moved through a "door in their consciousness," and more deeply understood the value of love and service. They also experienced greater insight on the impact they had upon the lives of those close to them. I have cared for others who, at the end of their lives, embraced family members they had not spoken to for many years. They inspired love in others, resolved personal issues that had troubled them for years, and died with a sense of inner accomplishment.

With some individuals, it seemed as though they were speaking to me and other family members and friends from a distant place during their final days — a place of self-knowing and inner peace. In these cases, the people were far removed from the relentless nature of the cancer or AIDS inhabiting their bodies. Ironically, for some, their disease involved the wasting of the physical form, and released the "armor" that had inhibited the spiritual aspect of their lives. This provided for a "rebirth" of their emotions and their spirits. What must life do to crack our physical "shell," and allow our emotional or spiritual self to "hatch"? For some people, the healing process helps bridge the boundary between the physical and the spiritual.

Sarah's Story

Sarah was a twenty-one-year-old orthodox Jewish woman who had just married into a family of prominent Israeli rabbis. Several months after her marriage, Sarah was diagnosed with ovarian cancer, and was treated with traditional therapies: chemotherapy and radiation.

When Sarah first came to my office for chiropractic care, she was very thin, and her distended belly made her appear as though she was eight months pregnant. Sarah was worried and depressed. She had given up hope for survival. As I cared for her over the next few months, I noticed that she had regained some strength and had started to smile. She began asking family and friends to visit her at home, and later in the hospital. She would often ask them to sing to her and tell jokes or stories to help lift her spirits.

Sarah was a child of Holocaust survivors. Her family had never spoken to their children about the horrors of the death camps; the emotional pain had been too much for them to deal with. One day, Sarah looked at the picture of her grandmother, "Bubbie," who had lost her life in Auschwitz. Her depression soon lifted, and was replaced by a burning desire to know more about the lives of her family. She especially wanted to know about her Bubbie. During the next few weeks, the last of her life, her father and mother told her the stories they had kept from her. Sarah also received phone calls from relatives and family friends living in Israel, South America, England, and other parts of the world. They told her stories about her family, especially her beloved Bubbie.

During this special time in her life, Sarah inspired her younger sister to sing, taught her mother to forgive, helped both her father and husband to live in the moment, and created an international community for herself. She died with greater strength, passion, and joy in her life, along with an inner knowing of who she was and why she was here on Earth. Accompanied by her grieving family,

Sarah's body was flown to Israel for burial. Over two thousand people came to her funeral, although she had never visited the Holy Land before. Healing occurred even though the outcome was not as all of us would have wished for.

Healing invites us to return to wholeness, regardless of the physical condition of our body. If given a choice of succumbing to disease without changing our perspectives, or succumbing to disease while attempting to heal our relationships with life, the choice is almost always toward healing. Healing will return us to wholeness, but *it does not always produce the outcome we desire.* Healing does not always mean that a particular symptom or disease will resolve itself, that our life expectancy will be extended, or that our pain will subside according to a schedule. As with Sarah, there are times when symptoms or circumstances cannot be fixed or corrected. It is especially in these moments that we can choose to heal. When it seems as though we cannot change the outcome of a situation or a condition in our body, we can receive them as they are.

. . . . *HEALING MAGIC* . . . .

My present situation is perfect for me. I can heal, regardless of my expected outcome. I hunger to better know the power that resides within me, and the love that I can express. I eagerly express the greatness that I am, and I share my love and greatness with others. I accept my life as a sacred journey that is guided by the power, wisdom, and strength of life itself.

· 17 ·

healing myth

Healing is predictable in its course.

Mary Beth lay in the hospital suffering from congestive heart failure and chronic liver disease. She was expected to die at any time, until she heard that Susie, her granddaughter, was ill and needed her help.

Mary Beth and Susie had a very special relationship. When Mary Beth realized that she was still needed, and her "work was not done," she experienced a remarkable recovery. She survived another three years, dying two months after she felt that Susie no longer needed her help.

Although the treatment of a particular condition may follow a predictable pattern, healing is remarkably unpredictable. Like the case of Mary Beth, I have frequently heard of a parent or grandparent having virtually no blood pressure, or having blood chemistries that would not support their being alive. By all medical standards, they were expected to have died, yet they waited hours or days until the "lost" child or grandchild appeared at the hospital bed. At times they waited until they could resolve a particular issue, or apologize to a family member for something they had done.

As we have seen, illness occurs when the body can no longer accommodate the blockage or inefficient flow of energy and information. If the blockage of energy is not addressed, the body's repertoire of responses to life's challenges is limited. In healing, the body becomes aware of the energy that has not been free to circulate, and the life force begins to flow more freely. Once the life force is flowing more freely, we can breathe more freely, and our state of consciousness changes.

In my years of clinical practice, I observed that even a small change in self-awareness, deeper respiration, or increased information exchange within the body can change our perceptions, influence our choices, and bring a new way of relating to ourselves and others. Many people gain new insights in their life, end toxic relationships and begin new ones, respond to stress differently, and embrace their personal power. These changes are more predictable and even expected by those living from the Tree of Life, but totally confusing to those eating only the fruit of the Tree of Knowledge.

As we heal, such unexpected outcomes are joyfully welcomed. This occurs in spite of the fact that healing causes us to say things we swore we would never say, do things we promised we would never do, and be with people we formerly wouldn't have been "caught dead with." As we establish new relationships with others, or with parts of our own bodymind, our whole life is affected. As a result, new experiences, including those which are life changing, begin to emerge. Our sometimes predictable direction in life undergoes a radical change as new insights are called into action that were not previously available. When healing takes place, it may change the course of our life, not only unpredictably, but radically.

. . . . *HEALING MAGIC* . . . .

The information and energy within me is now becoming "whole" again. As I acknowledge the parts of myself that have been ignored, isolated, suppressed, or forgotten, new and surprising insights spontaneously emerge from within me. These lead me to make new choices, help me to transform my relationships, and establish new ones. I joyfully welcome the unexpected outcome of this "new" me.

· 18 ·

healing myth

Healing takes time.

As an extension of the previous myth that "healing follows a predictable course," the myth that "healing takes time" can also be misleading. While it may be true that certain conditions, such as a broken leg, fractured skull, or hernia require a certain amount of time to mend, healing exists in a realm beyond time. Healing exists beyond thoughts and words, just as all miracles are beyond description. The outcome we seek may take time, but once the power of life expresses itself more fully, and moves through us more easily, healing is instantaneous.

If we tie a string around a branch of a plant, we block its energetic flow and interrupt the natural exchange of information between different parts of the plant. The result is withering leaves. Yet the moment we remove the string, healing occurs, even though it takes time for the leaves to revitalize. Similarly, healing instantly begins the second we make a more effective choice for ourselves, even though our body may not appear to be "fixed" or healed.

There is no other moment for healing except the present moment. We cannot heal in the past, since it no longer exists; we cannot heal in the future, because it isn't here yet. Healing occurs the instant a physical or mechanical obstruction is removed, or the instant we express our inner wisdom. Healing occurs the instant that parts of our body begin to share their stories with one another. Healing occurs the moment we liberate blocked energy that is stored in different areas of our body, or when our breath becomes more easy and natural. Healing occurs once we become more aware of our inner rhythms, once we smile more easily, and laugh more heartily. As our bodymind heals, we experience joyful moments more and more; we enjoy a greater sense of who we are, and celebrate the beauty and wonder in our life.

. . . . *HEALING MAGIC* . . . .

I am healing in this instant. I honor the healing that has already occurred, and I honor the healing that has yet to occur. Healing myself *now* is my gift to myself, to my family, and to my friends. Although my healing is instantaneous, it may take time before I fully experience the benefits.

· 19 ·

healing myth

Healing often requires drastic measures.

When we consider life with the logical mind alone, it makes sense that if we have a small problem, we might seek an easy solution requiring a minimum of energy or expense. If we are dealing with a major problem or crisis, we might expect the solution to be complex, difficult, expensive, or risky.

Let's consider this myth as it pertains to a study by the Arizona Cancer Center at the University of Arizona College of Medicine. In this six-year, double-blind study, participants taking selenium supplements had a 37 percent reduction of the incidence of cancer, and a 50 percent reduction of cancer mortality. Of the two hundred people studied, the group taking the selenium supplement had 63 percent fewer prostate cancers, 58 percent fewer colorectal cancers, and 46 percent fewer lung cancers than those taking a placebo. Not a single case of selenium toxicity was reported in any of the patients studied. Yet in the same issue of the *Journal of the American Medical Association* in which this study was published, dire warnings were asserted by the medical community telling patients not to use this all-natural, nutritional supplement. An editorial stated: "For now it is premature to change individual behavior, to market specific selenium supplements, or to modify public health recommendations based on the results of this one randomized trial."

I personally believe that had the study involved an expensive and dangerous treatment requiring extensive physician training, a high risk to patients, and an expensive hospital stay, the cultural mythos would have required the results of the study to be carried by the national media. Because the selenium represented such a simple, safe, and effective solution to a complex problem like cancer, the results were largely ignored by both the media and the medical community. After all, how can something so simple, inexpensive, and readily available help a person prevent such a complex, dangerous, and almost "incurable" condition, in spite of the billions of dollars spent per year in research by the finest minds in the world?

The Non-linear Approach to Wellness

While working within the chiropractic paradigm, I discovered the non-linear approach to wellness, and developed a form of "wellness care" known as Network Spinal Analysis (NSA). To my surprise, I found that a very gentle touch to the upper and lower spine can cause the entire spine to reconfigure itself. Deep respiration, along with wavelike undulations and dissipation of stored spinal tension are often associated with this gentle touch, and result in an overall enhancement of our quality of life. In the non-linear approach to wellness, a small change in our physiology produces a disproportionate response in our health and well-being. A strong force need not be applied to create a significant change in the bodymind. In fact, I discovered that applying a forceful touch can actually inhibit this process.

When I first developed Network Spinal Analysis, I found that memories of childhood hurts, accidents, or other physical or psychological traumas are often stored as tension and energy patterns in different parts of the body. This energy, confined under tension, is not unlike a powerful spring. Over time, it manifests in physically tight muscles, joint fixation, resistance to full body motion, depression, and shallow breathing. It also manifests as pain and disease.

I also observed that the more ill we are, the more energy we need to release in order to heal. The energy that is not free to circulate generates tension over time, until conditions are ripe for it to initiate the healing process. Hurts and wounds from our past build up pressure and "collect" energy from new hurts and wounds in the present. For example, our spouse makes a harmless remark about how we might have done something differently, and we respond with anger that lasts for several days. The remark sparks a reaction in the energy that is already "charged" by previous hurts or wounds. This energy becomes more and more blocked, denied, and isolated, until at last it is ready to be released. When the energy is released (or converted from a confined state into a freer state), it becomes available for healing, and actually helps fuel the healing process.

The non-linear approach to wellness considers the bodymind an interactive system, influenced by many factors that contribute to health or illness. The ability of our bodymind to receive, circulate, and dissipate energy, and our current and past experiences in life, significantly affect our health. In addition, our cultural story strongly influences how we interpret and respond to a given situation. The severity of the symptoms, the duration of a condition, or the degree of pathology do not by themselves determine the severity of the measures needed to be taken in order to heal. A small change, when perceived by the nervous system, can release the stored energy and tension, allowing it to be utilized by the body for constructive purposes like healing and transformation. When our bodymind becomes aware of the need for change, and can feel and pay attention to itself, there are many useful tools that facilitate self-awareness and act as a catalyst to enable old hurts or wounds to heal. A spinal adjustment, breathing exercises, a meditation practice, or yoga are just a few.

Healing neither requires great effort nor drastic measures. While curing or treating symptoms or disease may call for such measures, this is not the case with healing. As a byproduct of healing, we may decide to make radical changes in our life, but the decision to make such changes occurs as a result of the healing already in progress. It is by healing that we enhance our ability to make constructive changes.

. . . . *HEALING MAGIC* . . . .

I do not have to take drastic measures to heal. The energy that expresses itself as tension, pain, disease symptoms, or an unhappy, unfulfilled life is waiting for the opportunity to burst forth. I am ready to liberate this energy, to set it to work toward healing. I bless my symptoms, illness, and wounds because they are stepping-stones on my healing journey.

Notes

1. Bernard Lown, M.D., and Thomas N. Graboys, M.D., letter, *The New Yorker,* May 17, 1999.

2. *Journal of the American Medical Association,* Vol. 272, No. 23, December 21, 1994.

3. "Calcium Channel Blockers Under Fire," *Medical Sciences Bulletin,* April 1995.

4. Virginia Watson, "Annual Flu Shot for Seniors Debated," *Medical Tribune News Service,* May 22, 1997.

5. George Bergus, M.D., et al., "Antibiotic Use During the First 200 Days of Life," *Archives of Family Medicine,* October 1996.

6. Benjamin Schwartz, *Journal of the American Medical Association,* September 17, 1997.

Part 4

. . . .

Religious Myths

For many people, religion is the pathway to God, leading to experiences that fill them with awe, love, forgiveness, humility, and compassion. For others, religion — or their understanding of it — only hinders their appreciation of the sacred and the divine, especially when it engenders feelings of guilt and self-defeat.

Some of our most cherished healing myths come from religious ideology. Religious concepts that intend to guide individuals toward greater humility, selfless service to others, and salvation are frequently distorted by cultural interpretation. Although their intent may be to guide us on our spiritual path, religious myths — when taken out of a larger context, or when taken too literally — may hinder the healing process.

The myth that our physical body is inherently sinful or evil creates shame about ourselves and our bodies. It also suppresses our natural inclination to move or dance, to touch or be sensual, erotic, and ecstatic. Some religious myths not only suggest that the intellect must control our body's impure and "animalistic" urges, but that life itself cannot be trusted, and is punishment for our ignorance and past sins.

When we are ill, the belief that we are helpless victims of a situation we cannot control or even comprehend only aggravates our situation. The belief in a supreme patriarchal authority figure who judges and will punish us with eternal damnation at His whim (in most religious myths, God is depicted as "Him") can generate needless fear and feelings of despair. Believing we are condemned for our imperfections, or powerless to change our life circumstances, can discourage us from taking action to improve ourselves or our situation.

The religious concept that we must ask to be forgiven for the sins of the flesh to enter the divine or angelic realms assumes that we, as human beings, have already been condemned, and need to be forgiven. This myth can lead to permanent feelings of unworthiness and guilt when we feel we have not atoned for our sins, or forgiven others for theirs.

Within religious mythology, the truth of "the almighty" is so great, and the meaning of God so difficult to understand, that we need a hierarchy of priestly intermediaries to help us understand and interpret who God is and what God wants from us. Religious myths consider God's message to be so complicated that many years of study are required before we can possibly understand it. We are often told that the days of prophecy are over, so who are we to receive direct inspiration, messages, insights, or healing from the Lord? Eastern religions like Buddhism and Hinduism, and related spiritual practices like yoga, often encourage the elimination of the ego, pride, and desire. This may cause us to underestimate our own power, avoid reaching for our most cherished dreams, or sabotage our life with feelings of guilt. Achieving success (however one defines it), envisioning grand plans for ourselves, and becoming prosperous are incompatible with religious mythology.

Religious mythology is so deeply ingrained in our culture that we can easily fail to recognize its influence on our beliefs and behavior. To consider a few of these myths from a new perspective, let's begin by asking some questions:

- If we believe that God or Goddess is the Creator, do we trust in the creation that he or she has made?
- When a baby emerges from the womb, is its health so weak and fragile that it needs to be medicated, sanitized, and immunized against life in order to survive? To express this idea another way, does God stop creating us at birth?
- If we believe that God is the Creator *and* the Sustainer, why wouldn't we expect our body to heal and self-correct? Why fear disease or symptoms of ill health, rather than trust in our God-given body to heal?
- If we believe that God is the Redeemer, why should this apply only to our afterlife? Wouldn't it also apply to redemption for all ills and circumstances while we are still alive?

- Do we need to be abandoned as a child, swallowed by a whale, lost in the desert, turned into salt, nailed to a cross, experience every kind of plague, deny ourselves every physical pleasure, and die for our sins to prove ourselves worthy of God's love?

- Must we give up all of our possessions, do penance, or be celibate in order to receive joy, salvation, good health, and spiritual well-being?

Our religious ideology colors our stories about healing. Religious myths, like social and biomedical myths, tell us what the human bodymind is capable of, and what its limitations are in healing. Religious myths determine the way we view our personal role in the universe, the way we view authority figures, and what we can expect to experience on our journey toward health or healing. Our faith in certain myths may inhibit the expression of our inner voice and intelligence, which, as a reflection of the Divine, is meant to guide us through life.

It is not my intention to suggest that an individual's spiritual or religious beliefs are wrong or invalid. As with other myths discussed in this book, I am suggesting that a dogmatic adherence to certain religious myths may engender feelings of self-doubt, guilt, unworthiness, and low self-esteem. The physiology created by these feelings will only hinder the healing process.

· 20 ·

healing myth

Heaven is only available after this life.

This popular myth is taught in nearly every Sunday School class: Heaven is only available in the afterlife, and to enter heaven requires that we become a "good" person. What is meant by "good" could be any number of things, but only those who are deemed to be "good," or free of sin, will enter the realm of heaven. Our life on Earth will be judged by God, or the "highest court" with final determination for all of eternity.

This religious myth interferes with our right to experience heaven on Earth while we are physically alive. It suggests that the ability to experience divine love, absolution, ecstasy, and inner peace during our lifetime is unrealistic and may border on a loss of sanity, or a break with reality. Consequently, we don't expect to experience ecstasy, spiritual vision, or other attributes generally reserved for heaven while we are alive. If we accept the myth that heaven is only available in the afterlife, a problem will arise whenever we begin to experience the state of mind or body that brings us joy and bliss. Our thinking brain, together with our bodymind's conditioning, will deny the experience. Rather than the cerebral cortex (which controls the higher centers of brain function) encouraging these states of consciousness and producing the physiology that would support "heaven on Earth," we resort to a less blissful state, thus postponing the bliss of heaven until we die.

One woman, whom I knew through my clinical practice, struggled with this myth for many years. Maria had significant relationship difficulties stemming from her rejection of heaven on Earth. She strived to achieve the "perfect" relationship coupled with sublime sexual experiences, but whenever she experienced bliss after making love, she felt guilty. She would then create arguments, or break up with the man she loved. Whenever Maria was really happy, and pleasurable feelings began to flow through her, she felt guilty. In therapy, she discovered that she had been avoiding any experience of heaven, thus postponing the experience for her afterlife. Only then would such feelings be acceptable to her.

Do you believe it is possible to experience divine ecstasy, or heaven on Earth, in spite of your condition or circumstance? Do you believe that a person who has cancer, heart disease, or another serious ailment can still have joy in his life? If you believed it was possible to experience heaven on Earth, right now, would you be willing to postpone it?

. . . . *HEALING MAGIC* . . . .

I accept the state of consciousness known as "heaven," while living here and now. I know that my body and my life are sacred here and now. I honor my body and joyfully declare the presence of the Divine as it joins my life here on Earth. Today, regardless of my circumstance or situation, I choose to experience heaven.

· 21 ·

healing myth

Disease is a punishment for my sins.

This religious myth can inhibit the healing process because it promotes self judgment and blame for being sick. At the root of this myth is the belief that distressing situations in life are punishment for our sins. If you have an automobile accident, develop a disease, or lose a loved one, do you believe these events have happened to punish you for things you have done or not done? If your answer is yes, then healing through this event or circumstance will defy the Creator's will. Few beliefs can create a greater sense of helplessness, mental depression, and a weakening of the human spirit, than the one that God wants to punish us to "even the score."

Disease and symptoms are part of life and are not to be viewed as the result of our sins, failings, or imperfections. In his book, *Healing Words,* Larry Dossey, M.D., addresses this issue directly:

"We do not say that a tree is less a tree because it develops a cancer or is infested with borers. It is not a dog's fault that it develops hip dyplasia, and a cat is not innately defective because it comes down with feline leukemia. In nature, the occurrence of disease is considered a part of the natural order, not a sign of ethical, moral, or spiritual weakness."

Judging an illness or disease as God's punishment for wrong action or thought denies any benefits that may arise from the disease process itself, such as personal insights and other learning experiences.

Ethical conflicts, moral dilemmas, and personal conflicts contribute to biological conflict and lay the groundwork for disease. A person who lives her vision of life without inner conflict may be less prone to disease than a spiritually "awakened" individual who has high moral and ethical standards, but is always in conflict over the global significance of her personal choices.

Physical, emotional, mental, and chemical stresses placed upon us since birth, take a cumulative toll on our health and contribute to disease. An idealized self-image such as "supermom" or "nice guy" that we can never live up to, or other conflicts regarding cultural values we are expected to adopt, produce biological stress that can predispose us to disease. Mechanical tension on nerves, poor nutrition, hormonal, immunological, or other systemic stress can predispose us to disease, regardless of our religious beliefs, spiritual practice, or moral stance. All of these factors must be considered when we look at the basis of illness and disease.

The myth that "disease is a punishment for our sins" may be founded on the religious belief that we are born in sin and can only be redeemed after we die. If we are born in sin, or committed a terrible sin in this lifetime, what are we going to do for the rest of our life? Believing we have committed sins that cannot be forgiven during this lifetime hinders our potential for good health. Acknowledging inappropriate thoughts or actions is important, but becoming ill over what has already occurred serves no one. There is an old Hasidic adage that says: "He who has fallen furthest from God, God draws closest to his bosom, and he who is closest to God finds each step closer so very difficult." If a person believes he has sinned in the past, there is only one direction to go: forward. For those who consider themselves sinners, the desire to be drawn to the heart of our Creator can transform their physiology. The burning passion to serve others, and honor themselves in the process, can transform their lives and help them to heal.

Life promises renewal in every moment. Spring always follows winter's cold. The renewal of our physical body, which is being created in each moment, brings the possibility that our spirit, our mind, and our emotions can also be renewed in each moment. The belief in the renewal of life, in spite of our past, can lighten the burden of guilt we place upon ourselves and others. New cells are born every day within our physical body, replacing those cells that have died. Except for the nervous system, all of our body's cells will be replaced within two years, and we will have a totally new body. Are we going to condemn our "new" body for our past sins? By holding on to feelings of guilt for past sins, we store that vibration within our body, and continue to have that experience in the "new" body we are creating. Our past is our heritage and not our future destiny. The Lord's Prayer says, "Give us this day our daily bread." It does not refer to next week's bread, or to the bread that we baked years ago.

. . . . *HEALING MAGIC* . . . .

My symptoms, disease, or circumstance are not a punishment from God. They guide me to pay greater attention to the life force within me, so it can manifest with greater ease. I move forward in my healing, honoring myself and serving others. I rejoice in the fact that spring always follows winter, and give thanks for the healing that has brought me this realization.

· 22 ·

healing myth

I must forgive in order to heal.

During patient consultations, I would often ask, "If you feel you are ill, *why* do you feel you are ill?" It was not uncommon for patients who had a chronic or debilitating illness to report that they were not able to forgive someone who had hurt, abused, or injured them years before. Sometimes a patient would remark, "I know that if I could forgive him, I would begin to improve instantly."

Carol was receiving treatment for ovarian cancer in a local hospital. When I asked about what was really going on in her life, beyond the cancer, she said that she could not forgive the man who had raped her over twenty-four years before. She said that she would carry the scar he left on her until the day she died. Carol added that when she tried to forgive him, she felt a pain in her uterus along with a sense that she was further violating herself by trying to forgive him.

"I try, I hear the words in my head, but the feelings that come up are either nothing or anger, not forgiveness."

This particular religious myth, "I must forgive in order to heal," can also express itself as the need to be forgiven for our sins against God or our religion. Louisa had metastatic cancer and was in her final days. She remarked that she was frightened that she would not go to heaven because she was excommunicated from the Roman Catholic Church after her divorce fifty years before. She felt that neither the Church nor God would forgive her for having been divorced and subsequently marrying outside her religion. This hurt still lingered, though she had a loving and deeply committed relationship with her husband of almost half a century.

One day, a Lutheran clergy member told her that God would surely have absolved her due to her loving commitment to her second husband and their family. Upon hearing this, Louisa laughed and cried, saying that she deeply yearned to be with the rest of her loved ones in heaven. She then felt that whenever she died she would be reunited with the Lord rather than punished. Louisa was ready to allow forgiveness. She had already healed enough to invite the minister into her life to affirm what she wanted and needed to hear: that she was forgiven.

Respecting Biological Readiness

Imagine meeting someone who is attractive, charming, wealthy, and fulfills every criterion your intellect tells you would make the perfect mate. There is only one problem: Although you like this person, there is no sense of magic or feeling of "Oh my God, my knees are weak when I hear his voice or feel her touch." Although the intellect may steer us in a particular direction, it is our physiology that determines whether we feel passion, ecstasy, and love. Our physiology also brings us the ability to experience spontaneous, complete, and profound forgiveness.

The act of forgiving ourselves and others can have a powerful effect on the healing process. I have witnessed crippled people begin to walk, deaf people hear again, people in pain for years breathing with ease, broken relationships mend, and personal creativity, intellectual growth, and business success blossom after they unconditionally forgave themselves and others. The timing, however, is determined by our physiology, as opposed to our intellect. According to the story from the Tree of Knowledge, the thinking mind chooses what we do and when, and this includes forgiveness. Yet forgiveness does not happen according to a timetable created by the mind alone.

In her story, Carol stated it perfectly when she said, "I try, I hear the words in my head, but the feelings that come up are either nothing or anger, not forgiveness." She reported that she felt like she was lying to herself when she tried to forgive him, and she was right. Forgiveness is the culmination of an energetic, biological process dictated by the Tree of Life. It is time to forgive when the information and energy involving a particular person or event has been received by both the mind and the body. When the energetic message has been revealed to our entire bodymind, not just the intellect, we no longer need to hold on to the tension associated with this part of our life. Forgiveness is experienced by what I call "biological readiness," rather than convenience or logic.

. . . . *HEALING MAGIC* . . . .

I am open to forgiveness for myself and for others whenever the timing is right for me. Today, I celebrate the forgiveness that has spontaneously sprung forth in my life, and I honor the healing that has already occurred. For those I have not yet forgiven, I trust that forgiveness will come as my bodymind heals.

· 23 ·
healing myth

The self or ego is the cause of distress or disease.

Our *self* is the essential part of our nature that makes us different from everyone and everything else. According to Dr. Roberto Assagioli, the developer of a psychological modality known as Psychosynthesis, the self is acutely aware of itself as a distinct and separate individual. In Western tradition, the lack of a sense of self, or fixation of the development of self, is viewed as the basis of psychopathology. In Eastern spiritual tradition, it is common to consider the surrender of ego, or one's illusionary sense of self, a necessity when treading the path to enlightenment.

"To self or not to self" is a question we might ask ourselves, but our true self or ego is not the cause of our distress or disease. Instead, it is the "false" sense of self or the "inflated" ego that may cause distress or disease. If who or what we identify with were threatened, damaged, or lost, would we become ill or express symptoms of disease? If the answer is "yes," then we have incorporated this identity into a "false" sense of self or ego. This does not make us right or wrong, but it clearly describes what has happened.

An example of a "false" sense of self would be identification with our accomplishments in life. Some people act as if they *are* their profession or their political party, or identify themselves with their spouse or children. Some incorporate their likes and dislikes, personal possessions, or religion into their sense of self. They declare: "I am a vegetarian," "I am a Christian," "I am an investment banker," or "I am Sam's wife." Saying "I choose to eat vegetables instead of meat" is a different statement than "I am a vegetarian." "I am married to Sam" is different from saying "I am Sam's wife." In truth, we are not our religion, our profession, or our political party. During our lifetime we may align ourselves with certain philosophies, people, or practices, but if our spouse, job, religion, or philosophy were to change, we would still be our "self." Therefore, we need to be aware of the words we place after "I am."

Who we think we are, or "our ego" is often what insulates us from an awareness of our inner self. The "inflated" ego, just like the "false" sense of self, can come from a lack of understanding of our true nature. There is a self, or being, that is beyond the limited view we normally accept about ourselves. That self or being is connected to every other being. What we consider our "private" thoughts, feelings, and experiences are felt by others also. Although the "sense of self" may lead to a sense of solitude or separation from the world around us, in truth the self is never separate from the entire community of beings, or from nature itself.

We are separate from others, and yet we are inseparable, and as long as we live through this physical body, we will never resolve this paradox. The more we look within us, the more we find what is also outside of us. The more we look outside of us, the more we find what is also within. All healing is the natural result of the flow and dance of energy between these two realms.

When exploring self or ego-related issues, the following questions may be of value in surrendering the "false" sense of self to a more integrated sense of being:

- Who am I?
- Is "who I am" or my "sense of self" interfering with my health or my happiness?
- Do I need to relinquish my self or ego in order to attain happiness?
- Is my life focused on the accumulation of wealth, titles, or material things?
- If I am selfless or "ego-less," can I still have desires and dreams?
- Is my health influenced by my successes or failures in life?

. . . . *HEALING MAGIC* . . . .

I joyfully acknowledge both my inner "self," and the "me" I see in the mirror. I smile as I realize that little of what I thought was "me" is true about myself. I celebrate who and what I am, and who and what I am not. I reclaim my new sense of "self," my identity, and renew my passion for healing by saying "yes" to life.

· 24 ·

healing myth

The days of prophecy are over;
messages from the divine are not available to me.

At the core of many world religions is a story of a sacred transmission or communication between the Divine and the central figure or figures of that religion. Historically, it is common for a limited group of religious leaders or scholars to decide whether a divine or mystical communication, vision, or voice has true spiritual significance. This small group of religious figures will then interpret the original message for the masses, and for the many generations to come.

According to the myth that "the days of prophecy are over," only a handful of individuals over a period of thousands of years can be eligible for divine insight or prophecy. Any insights or spiritual communications received by the masses are false, dangerous, and unworthy of our trust. The rare individual who does consider his message one of Divine intervention must endure the scrutiny of those ordained authority figures who are highly educated in the ways of the Lord, and schooled in the appropriate ways to evaluate the event.

Therefore, regardless of the validity of true Divine insight, visitation, or prophecy, we are trained to doubt the possibility of such experiences in our lifetime. Furthermore, we are taught that we lack the spiritual faculties to understand the message. We doubt the messages we might receive through light (as in the biblical story of the burning bush), sound (as in the voice of angels), or the sensory experience of love. When we feel compelled to pay attention to such experiences, we are in physiological conflict. By silencing our inner voice, we lose the connection to our inner rhythms and pulsations. At the same time, we fear those internal sensory experiences that overwhelm us, place us out of control, or are "powerfully spiritual" in nature.

Perhaps our burning arm or aching leg, the heaviness in our chest, the tightening of our muscles or joints, or different forms of visceral distress are due to a scrambling of messages of divine insight or prophecy about our own life. Once energy and information is circulating through the bodymind, where might it go if it were powerful enough to inspire generations to come, or change the course of human history? Might it seem that something is really "wrong" with us if we have condemned the possibility of divine revelation within ourselves?

When we are trapped in life, feel helpless to change our situation or disease, or believe the odds are against us, isn't that when we ask for God's intervention and wisdom the most? Are we prepared for the possibility that we may have indeed received the message? Might our present situation be at least partially the result of not having sanctified these energetic messages in the past?

A Parable of the Religious Man

A religious man was trapped in his home by flood waters caused by a powerful hurricane. He considered the situation strange, because he had experienced a recurring dream about this disaster for several weeks. In his dream, God had saved his life.

As the water rose to the second story of his home, he awaited God's salvation. A small motorboat approached his home, and the boatman called out, "You in there, come on out; come to safety on my boat." The religious man refused, waiting for God to save him, and for the flood waters to subside. Shortly after this encounter, the water level reached the top floor of his house, and a raft floated by. The people on board offered him a ride, but again, he said, "No thank you," while waiting for the Lord to help him. Finally, as the man was standing on the roof of his home, a helicopter dropped a rope to save him from the rising waters. Once more he rejected the offer, while awaiting the help of God. Shortly afterward, he drowned. Upon entering heaven, he asked the angels why God had not saved him. They answered that God had spoken to him with a prophecy in his dreams. Then God sent a motorboat, a raft, and a helicopter to save him from drowning. Each time, the man had refused God's help.

In this story, the man believed he had received God's message through his dreams, but his own expectations kept him from receiving God's gift. The man may have considered himself worthy of divine intervention, but he did not realize that it can come in many forms. In this instance, it came to him through the form of other people who offered to save his life.

. . . . *HEALING MAGIC* . . . .

God communicates with me in many ways. I receive divine messages through my dreams, intuition, and relationships with others. Divine messages may appear as sound, light, images, and emotion. In faith, I receive messages that are broadcast from the Divine. I rejoice in the communications I am given, and celebrate the gifts received through experiences that deviate from my usual patterns and routines.

· 25 ·

healing myth

*Uninhibited expressions of the human body
are not as sacred as religious prayer.*

Religious mythology often places the power of God outside of ourselves, instead of within us. The human body is considered "less holy"
than the human spirit, however, it is only *through our body* that we can
express spirit or the essence of God. It is only through a more profound *attentiveness to our body* that we can truly honor our spiritual
self, and transform our experience of life.

God's name or a specific prayer will not heal us more than the
free expression of emotion, movement, and breath. Every thought,
emotion, and feeling has a unique vibrational state or frequency. It is
the body that maintains the frequency that allows us to resonate with
a particular emotion, or to have any experience. Therefore, we can
honor our spiritual nature, along with our divine God or Goddess
attributes, through a greater attentiveness to the pulsations, rhythms,
patterns of tension and ease, and vibrations of our body.

In this religious myth, it is not the power of prayer that I am questioning, but the religious concept that the human body is not sacred or divine. Prayer places our attention on the presence and importance of the Divine in our life. It helps us connect to a plane of consciousness from which it is believed a spiritual force can work its miracles more effectively in our life. Petitionary prayer, in which we ask the Almighty for a specific favor, action, or intervention, is not unlike the individual who discovers a magic lamp possessing a genie. Expressions like, "Lord, please make this problem go away," or "God, please protect me from this circumstance, person, or condition," are forms of petitionary prayers. In this type of prayer, a part of us that feels helpless, isolated, or afraid, is asking for help. Yet that part of us that petitions God for assistance is often not whole enough to know what to ask for. As a result, what we ask for is often a temporary solution to our problem, and does not always satisfy us on a deeper level.

That is why I believe the most sacred type of prayer is one that comes through natural and uninhibited rhythms, vibrations, and movements of the body. For some people, writhing in pain and holding a particular part of the body is the only way to begin to sanctify the body and its gifts. Moaning, crying, calling out in ecstasy, or laughing uncontrollably can all be forms of prayer. By moving our body rhythmically, a respiratory pattern naturally emerges, inviting divergent energies to coexist in harmony. In this state, our prayer reflects who we are, where we have been, and what we have done. It is profound in its organic nature, and provides a powerful means of sanctifying our wounds and stories about ourselves.

The human body is a sacred temple. Through the Divine, we have been given a body as the means of experiencing life and honoring God. No other person can tell us how to express our devotion to spirit through our body, and only we and the Divine know the meaning of its expression.

. . . . *HEALING MAGIC* . . . .

I celebrate the union of body and spirit. Through movement, breath, and the compassionate touching of my body, I gain insight into myself. By sanctifying my body, I open the door to healing. I take time out from all my activities, preoccupations, or thoughts, to honor my body and to pray a new and ancient prayer to my Creator's gift to me.

·26·

healing myth

Silence will heal me.

A friend of mine once told me that her silent time during the day was essential to her health and spiritual practice. I asked her if silence was necessary for her to heal. Her answer was, "Of course." If silence was necessary to heal, what would happen to her physiology when she is in the middle of a city, filled with noisy, frenetic activity? Would her bodymind, therefore, be programmed to become ill?

Silence and stillness certainly have a beneficial effect on us. In silence, we can hear our own inner voice, as well as the calming sounds of the natural world. However, I know of people who feel ill when they become silent. Certain individuals cannot tolerate quiet in their home, activities, or relationships. In the quiet moments after lovemaking, for instance, they feel compelled to begin a discussion, light a cigarette, drink a cup of coffee, or further stimulate their minds and bodies. As long as these people are occupied and can thrust themselves in the middle of the action, they feel well. They are also more productive, experience more joy in life, and are more fun to be with. For such people, is activity and noise healing?

In my years of clinical practice, I sometimes encountered patients, especially those who had a history of severe trauma, who did not want any music playing, including soft or gentle sounds, during their office visit. To the dismay of others who believed the soothing music helped them to heal, they would ask for the music to be turned off. These people retreated to a silent space within themselves to be comfortable and to heal. They did not want to be distracted by any sounds coming from the external environment.

I have seen patients resist moaning, groaning, crying out loud, or having their voice heard by others, even when it might have helped them to acknowledge and dissipate energy and information locked within a region of their body. They would often get angry or silently cry when other patients moaned, cried, or yelled out loud. In a group dynamic, the sounds and movements repressed by one person will often be expressed by another in the same group. This is their energetic gift to us, although at times it does not seem like a gift at all, but an annoyance. At times, the individuals who preferred silence would find themselves suddenly out of control; their personal noise and chaos would explode from within, setting them free to reach a new level of peace and inner stillness. Then the cycle would repeat itself, and they would prefer total silence.

Silence and stillness, noise and activity, each bring us their gifts and challenges. Living life away from noise and activity, or living life in the midst of noise and activity are personal preferences. At different times, each one may be more effective for healing. The story we create about what is appropriate or not, what is natural and not, and what is necessary for healing is often more important than the actual circumstance in which we find ourselves. Perhaps there is no such thing as a natural and unnatural world, because what is natural and what is not? A part of nature cannot be separated from the rest of nature, and we, as a creation of nature, cannot produce something outside of nature.

Silence does not heal. Music does not heal. Noise does not heal. *We* heal. It is essential to place the power where it belongs, and the power lies within us. The power is in the force of nature utilized by our bodymind in every moment of our lives.

. . . . *HEALING MAGIC* . . . .

Nature helps me to heal, whether it is noisy or silent. I may prefer to retreat from noise and activity, or I may choose noise and activity to activate my healing. I am grateful for the many ways in which the power within me uses noise within the stillness, and stillness within the noise to heal me. I can heal in any environment, because nothing exists outside of nature.

Part 5

. . . .

New Age Myths

"The New Age" or "The Age of Aquarius" has brought about exciting trends in human consciousness in the past forty years. These include a "new" view of the unity and interrelatedness of life, a desire to heal the rift between humans and our social and physical environments, and the questioning of old paradigms relating to government, business, education, and religion. The New Age has also been marked by important developments in equal rights for women and minorities, and has spawned innovative ways to liberate human potential.

Central to New Age thought is the belief that we "create" the major events in our life through our individual intent, thoughts, feelings, and will. Taking personal responsibility for our actions is important; however, when this New Age ideal is viewed through the perspective of old mythologies, serious distortions can result. This idea is often presumed to mean that we are personally responsible for contracting a serious illness, or for a hurricane destroying our home. Improper thought, or "impure" emotional energies, are associated with difficult times, and proper use of our mental faculties are associated with more pleasant ones. In these instances, New Age mythology has become a modern variation of the Tree of Knowledge, suggesting that we can control our environment with the "correct" use of our thinking mind.

Those who subscribe to New Age myths often have a secular and heightened sense of personal importance in the creation of natural phenomena and global trends. Statements are often made about the connection between events and circumstances and the individual's will or "psychic energy." For example, the occurrence of a lightning storm may be thought to signify the electrical charge in a personal relationship, or to reflect feelings of anger that an individual is holding. I have heard people report that toxic chemicals and electromagnetic radiation will not affect them, as long as they bless their personal crystal and charge it with love. If those people should feel anger, resentment, or greed, it is perfectly reasonable to expect the "negative forces" in the world to gain control of their lives once again.

The desire to willfully transcend negative emotions, avoid confrontation, and let sweet and loving energies prevail, are central to many who consider themselves a part of the New Age movement. Individual self-expression, along with an emphasis on the repressed inner child also underscore New Age mythology. In a desire to avoid confrontation and to freely express oneself, qualities like discipline, structure, and personal sacrifice are rarely encouraged, because they infringe upon what "feels good." This adolescent-like attitude is frequently associated with mistrust and resentment of authority, power, status, and wealth. New Age myths encourage a worldview that is often at odds with the achievement of success. The idea that spirituality and abundance are incompatible is commonly expressed in this popular story.

New Age myths encourage the individual to develop avoidance strategies for anything that does not "feel right." Decisions are made according to what *does* feel right, and bodily sensations are often confused with messages from our higher self or spiritual awareness. In the New Age story, it is sometimes said that since God created everything, and God participates in everything, then the individual *is* God. Although this logic may appear to make sense, I see it as an attempt to overemphasize our importance in the world. Just because the moon's image is reflected in a glass of water that we drink doesn't mean the moon is the water.

Part of the New Age story teaches that the feminine, or nurturing, side of humanity is the answer to society's problems. Many who embrace this story impart a type of New Age bigotry that is traditionally associated with patriarchy or male bigotry. By rejecting the male, human qualities considered masculine, such as discipline and structure, are devalued. At the same time, great importance is placed on one's childlike, free-spirited nature, often at the expense of the mature adult.

New Age mythology offers a radical departure from other mythologies in this book because it calls for respect and compassion for the spirit of life and the consciousness behind all form. It seeks to embrace the child within us, along with our feelings. New Age mythology also assumes that the individual has a special place in the world, and encourages us to create a greater synthesis of spirit, mind, emotions, and body. For these reasons and more, it may empower the individual and the healing process. Yet for other reasons, some of which are outlined on the following pages, New Age mythology can inhibit the healing process.

By questioning these New Age myths, I am not criticizing all New Age ideology. I only wish to question dogmatic beliefs that have outlived their usefulness, and challenge the New Age mythologies rooted in the Tree of Knowledge. Many consider the New Age movement as a bridge to a new mythology that is still evolving within our culture. In time, this new mythology will hopefully break free from its emphasis on the Tree of Knowledge, and more fully embrace the Tree of Life.

· 27 ·

healing myth

I am responsible for creating my reality.

This myth lies at the core of New Age mythology, and is the "motto" of many who consider themselves part of the New Age community. The concept of creating our reality runs counter to the idea that we are powerless in the world, and encourages people to take responsibility for their lives. If we do not like our current situation, we know that something can be done to create a better life. As a result, this idea generates a sense of personal power and attentiveness to our daily habits and activities. It may also help lead our culture from old stories of the past millennium into new stories, but adherence to the spell of this myth may be detrimental to our health because it is rooted in the Tree of Knowledge.

I recently spoke about this myth at a public lecture. At the end of the talk, a woman in a wheelchair maneuvered herself toward me with tears streaming down her face. She blurted out, "Thank you!

Thank you! Thank you!" and took my hand in hers and kissed it. She went on to say that she was an incest survivor, and had asked herself why she created her stepfather having sexual relations with her for eight years. She was tormented over why she had created her son committing suicide, why she had created her uterine cancer, a hysterectomy, a divorce, the tornado that destroyed her Texas home, and finally, her multiple sclerosis.

The woman reported that over the past twenty years, she felt progressively guilty and helpless over a series of violations that had happened to her. She bought this myth "hook, line, and sinker," and sink she did. Bringing the power of this story into her life made her feel responsible for situations and events that were largely beyond her control. The possibility of tremendous damage to the body's energetic systems — including the immune system and the nervous system — is set into motion when we experience feelings of helplessness for a prolonged period. Blocking the expression of our life energy and spirit by adhering to such a mythos does nothing to advance the healing process.

In my lecture, I referred to this New Age story as a myth. I said that although we set forces into motion that can influence certain outcomes, many circumstances are apparently independent of our volition, actions, or desires. At times, the main "lesson" seems to center on how the universe does *not* personalize events. Certain events occur with us or without us; in fact, they often happen *in spite of us*. The woman reported that when I made these statements, she felt as though a heavy weight was removed from her chest, head, and legs. She told me something magical had happened to her during the talk:

Her thinking was changing, and for the first time in over twenty years she did not feel like "a waste of humanity, a worthless piece of flesh." She looked deep into my eyes as she held my hands and said, "It is not for me to create my reality. No, it is not. It is for me to experience what I experience, without having to judge or make up a story about it."

I don't know what happened in this woman's life after that evening. I don't know if she regained the use of her legs, although becoming ambulatory would not be "proof" of her healing. I suspect that she was becoming more whole for the first time since her childhood. The powerful forces of healing that occur as we create a new story would at least dispel some of her darkness.

To think that the sun, moon, and stars, and all of nature revolve around our thoughts and desires is self-centered and narcissistic. It is also naive to believe that our immediate thoughts and actions, or inactions, create all that happens to us. The bodymind is influenced by all that we have been, all that we have done, all that we have believed, and all that we have interacted with. The bodymind is influenced by countless elements within our natural environment — past, present, and future. Our actions, and even our inactions, can be compared to wavelike messages sent into the universe at large. These mix with and overlap those waves set into motion by all other beings. What we experience as our "reality" could be said to be the sum total of all wave interference patterns.

It is important that we take responsibility for our life and that we fully *experience our experience*. When we say we are responsible for creating our reality, what we mean is that we create the *internal state* that witnesses and experiences the world. Our internal state is the reality we are responsible for. We are responsible for gaining a greater ability to experience how our body feels in response to outer circumstances, as well as to thoughts, ideas, or feelings that float through our mind. We are responsible for the state of tension, pain, or ease that we feel in our bodymind.

As we wake up and pay attention to what is going on within and around us, our inner state will move toward greater ease. Life will begin to flow more easily, and other people will respond to us differently. To the degree that we develop our awareness, we become "lucky" in life. Yet waking up, paying attention, and fully experiencing our experience needn't be for the sole purpose of changing our circumstances or attaining our desires. Instead, we can choose to allow the powers of attraction and creation to manifest whatever is consistent with who we are now, and who we can be in the future. Then the impact of various events, whether pleasant or unpleasant, may be viewed from a new perspective — a new and different story that we *do* create.

· · · · · · · · · · · · *HEALING MAGIC* · · · · · · · · · · · ·

I am not responsible for creating my external reality. I am responsible for my internal state of mind, emotion, and vibration. I am responsible for focusing my attention on my inner environment in relationship to my life circumstances. It is my gift to become aware of the state of tension, pain, or ease in my bodymind, and to accept my experiences — pleasant or unpleasant — with nonjudgment and love.

· 28 ·

healing myth

I must "open my heart" in order to heal.

Many "New Agers" are familiar with the Hindu concept of the seven *chakras*, or energy centers of the body. When a chakra is open, the type of energy transmitted or received will correspond to the qualities represented by each chakra: survival, sexuality, will, love, expression, thought, and spiritual vision. When an energy center is closed or otherwise blocked, we are cut off from the particular energy represented by that chakra.

The Seven Chakras

Many people who profess a belief in New Age mythology elevate the "heart center" above all other energy centers of the body, except perhaps the "crown" chakra, which is associated with spiritual vision and realization. In New Age mythology, all things that are worthy of admiration, or draw people together, are attributed to the "higher" energy centers. The "lower" energy centers connected to survival, sexuality, and personal power are often looked down upon or considered less desirable. In the quest to develop a more compassionate, heart-centered world, other vital aspects of human expression, such as sexual magnetism from the "lower" energy centers, are rejected in favor of the "higher" ones. Yet people who express themselves through their "lower" energy centers often exude an energy that is exciting, passionate, creative, and enjoyable.

Generally speaking, people are not attracted to others who express themselves mostly from an "open heart," unless the "lower" energy centers are also open. We may speak of a "heart connection" with someone, but an energetic exchange with others involves a combination of chakras. What we truly mean is that our entire physiology enjoys being near this person. Maybe we feel intellectual rapport, or greater self-acceptance and self-love when he or she is near. We may also feel sexually aroused in the other person's presence. Other energy centers are engaged, and our attraction is not limited to the heart center. Having a discussion with a loved one, for example, involves the heart center and thought center. Passionately speaking our truth involves the heart and throat chakras. Expressing our feelings about community, or sharing our global vision, activates the heart and crown centers. Sharing difficult times requiring the force of will along with compassion activates the heart center and solar plexus. When expressing romantic and sexual love, energy from the heart chakra and the root chakra are called into play.

"Opening our heart" may enhance our feelings of compassion and unconditional love, but it only transmits a fragment of our self. Without integrating the other energetic centers of the body, we cannot effectively manifest love or a sense of wholeness. At times, we may need to allow the sexual center to become more energetically alive and integrated with the rest of the bodymind in order to heal. The power chakra, near the center of the body, may need to be activated to reclaim our personal power in life. The throat chakra may need to express itself more than other energy centers when we need to communicate with both thought and feeling. Willfully planning to create changes inspired by the power of life may require the brow chakra to be activated. The crown center may need to be awakened to help us gain new insights associated with greater healing.

There are times when we may even need to express "raw" sexuality, anger, or power in order to heal. When this occurs, it is common for the bodymind to direct attention away from the heart center and open or awaken other energy centers needed in healing. The opening or awakening of an energy center can be uncomfortable, stressful, and even painful at times; when the alienated vibrations of our feelings are finally expressed, symptoms or illness often appear. If this occurs, we are likely to seek treatment, which may result in the energy center closing, and making us feel comfortable once more.

As we continue to heal, all energy centers of the body begin to open or awaken, and become more available. Thus, an "opening of the heart" is a byproduct of healing, rather than a cause of it.

· · · · · · · · · · · · *HEALING MAGIC* · · · · · · · · · · · ·

I celebrate the participation of all physical, energetic, and spiritual centers of my body. I place my hands on each center, gently breathe into each area, and experience my body rising and falling in that region. My body resonates with love for every part of my bodymind, and broadcasts this energy through my being and into the world.

· 29 ·

healing myth

Being highly evolved means no longer having negative emotions.

What New Age enthusiasts call "negative emotions" are feelings that are unpleasant to experience, such as grief, anger, frustration, and rage. When experienced over a prolonged period, these emotional states can be harmful to our health, yet all emotions are a natural part of the dance of consciousness and flow of energy in the body. The concept of "positive" or "negative" emotions is meaningless when we consider that the word *emotion* simply refers to "energy in motion." What people call "negative emotions" are more often the result of an inability to *express* emotion. Energy that cannot be expressed is stuck or held within a confined region of our bodymind.

Often we are not aware that a part of our bodymind is grieving, angry, or enraged. This may be especially true when we consider an emotion "negative." The emotion is pushed to the "back" of our mind, and when it shows up as back pain, arthritis, asthma, colitis, or angina, we do not associate the condition with our emotions, or with energy that is unexpressed, disconnected, or blocked from moving freely. We do not associate these problems with body tissues that are not responding to the demands of the moment. Nor do we connect disease to tension in the spine, back, and associated tissues and organs of the body.

Whenever an emotion is inhibited or blocked, this creates an energetic and structural state that I refer to as an *attitude* (a term I have borrowed from Ida P. Rolf, Ph.D., the developer of a healing modality known as Structural Integration, or Rolfing). A person who has an *attitude* uses it to distance himself from his emotions. Attitudes are associated with lack of flexibility of body tissues, lack of motion and vibration in at least one area of the body, and a lack of respiration into a part of the spine (which houses the switchboard regulating the relationship between the brain and the body).

The vibrational, energetic, and tension patterns from our past experiences maintain an "after-image" or physical imprint in the bodymind. Residue from past traumas becomes body tissue, and life energy that is unable to move through its full range of motion cannot express consciousness that is greater than the *attitude* in that region. Attempting to eliminate this energy or keep it from sharing its story with the rest of us only causes the energy to build up once again, possibly with greater intensity. The only way to avoid this situation is to develop a relationship with the energy and tension that have become isolated and ignored. By so doing, we allow it to be transformed into useful energy that can assist in our healing.

In the bodymind, whenever any two parts of a system relate to each other, new properties emerge that increase our awareness and help us to "evolve." Every new relationship between various physical and emotional components affects the entire bodymind. The more our bodymind evolves, the more information we instantly process. The healthier bodymind can make choices more rapidly because its component parts share information and dissipate energy and tension more efficiently. The healthy bodymind can be aware of tension and ease, but it doesn't have to react to it. Each part of the bodymind can do its job, share energy, and release what isn't needed at the moment.

As our bodymind evolves, we enjoy more freedom of motion, greater energy flow, and the awareness to distinguish the difference between having more or less energy flow. In addition, we have a greater capacity to explore information and energy that was previously unavailable or invisible to us. Just as a microscope amplifies objects and offers information that was formerly invisible, being "more highly evolved" may offer a greater amplification of energy in all realms of life, including the physical, emotional, mental, and spiritual. Through the amplification of energy and information, we receive greater understanding and a unique perspective. The more aware or "evolved" person will experience trapped or noncirculating energy (energy that another person might call the remnant of past traumas or negative emotions) more deeply than another. That person, however, will not consider it negative, but instead, just "energy," and a doorway to greater freedom.

The bodymind naturally experiences a wide range of vibrational states and their associated biochemistry as the body tissues move through their full range of motion. This is akin to having a satellite dish capable of receiving a huge number of channels or broadcasts. Difficulty arises when we choose certain stations at the expense of others, or when we keep responding to an earlier broadcast even though we have now changed channels. (That is, when our repertoire of response is basically the same regardless of our need for adaptation). It is as though we react with "feeling upset," when feeling gratitude and love might be a more appropriate response. This occurs because our physiology is tuned to the station "W-UPSET," no matter what our attention is focused on.

In *Molecules of Emotion*, Candace Pert, Ph.D., describes the chemical, physical, emotional, and spiritual dance that constantly takes place within our bodymind. She proposes that a particular emotion is associated with a corresponding vibration of "peptides," which are similar to a string of small amino acids (the "building blocks" of protein). It is suggested that as the peptide approaches the surface of a cell, a mutual harmonic vibration (oscillation) occurs that enhances the peptide's ability to bind on the surface of the cell. The structural or energetic architecture of the surface of the cell changes, and a particular peptide in circulation is given a "parking spot" on the cell. Once the peptide "parks" and enters the home of the cell, it changes the way the cell functions and "moves energy." Each vibrational state or characteristic movement of energy is believed to be experienced as a specific emotion. When the peptide does not reach the cell, when it is not recognized by the cell, or when it doesn't find a suitable "parking spot," the characteristic biochemical and energetic changes associated with that emotion do not occur, and that emotion will not be expressed.

Try this experiment. Sit with your arms placed in front of you. Project feelings of anger into your right arm. Do this until you can sense angry feelings in your right arm. Now relax without anger, and project feelings of love into the left arm. Do this until you feel relatively sure you have accomplished the task. Relax again. Next, try to place anger in the right arm, and love in the left arm, at the same time. Were you able to do it? The emotions of love and anger are mutually exclusive. We can experience one or the other, or move quickly between both states, but we cannot feel both emotions simultaneously. Perhaps future research will discover that love and anger are mutually exclusive experiences because they compete for the same "parking spot" on the cell.

. . . . *HEALING MAGIC* . . . .

I evolve as I become aware of the different parts, energies, and relationships of my bodymind. I heal as all of my parts share their stories with one another without judgment. I transform as I experience the energy and tension that has been isolated and ignored. There is no such thing as a "negative" emotion; there is only information and energy that is now made available for me to heal.

· *30* ·

healing myth

People who are "enlightened" do not experience disease.

This healing myth associates enlightenment with the ability to transcend negative circumstances, disease, and even "negative karma." Enlightened individuals are assumed to have achieved a perfect union of physical and spiritual existence, and to never be thrown off balance by circumstance. In contrast, it is assumed that an "unenlightened" person is more vulnerable to physical ailments and disease.

If we ascribe to the Tree of Knowledge, being ill is not compatible with spiritual enlightenment. Yet it isn't true that spiritually enlightened people do not contract diseases or have ailments. Many of the world's most revered spiritual leaders, including Mother Teresa, Sri Ramana Maharshi, and J. Krishnamurti, suffered some disease toward the end of their lives. The enlightened person will regard her ill health or negative situation as a gift, knowing that it also serves her spiritual path. In many cases, her condition serves to encourage her to seek further awareness, spiritual growth, and enlightenment.

I have met many individuals who were considered by their devotees and students as having attained enlightenment, or close to it, in this lifetime. Some had experienced degenerative changes due to life-threatening illnesses like cancer, diabetes, and heart disease. Others had considerable pain. I have personally provided Network Spinal Analysis care to several of these masters.

I have also heard of gurus or spiritual teachers who "take on the karma" of their disciples and consequently develop disease. In this case, disease is chosen because the gurus feel that by accepting the discordant energy of their disciples, they can transmute it to a higher level. This is a selfless act; however, the guru may deny the disciples the opportunity to learn the lessons to be gained from working with their own discordant energy and the disease symptoms that arise. Enlightenment is not only the ability to enjoy the "game of life," but a willingness to inspire others to fully participate in the game.

. . . . *HEALING MAGIC* . . . .

I am becoming aware of my internal energies, rhythms, feelings, and thoughts. Greater joy and enlightenment are a bonus of this awareness. I regard my symptoms and disease as a gift with valuable lessons to share with me. Being present with, and accepting all of my gifts, is the path to enlightenment.

· 31 ·

healing myth

Profound new awareness is necessary in order to heal.

If our goal in life is to learn new lessons according to the Tree of Knowledge, then one would expect that "new awareness" is necessary in order to heal. Profound new awareness would especially be required to heal ourselves of major diseases and difficult situations in life. By contrast, only a little knowledge or awareness would be necessary to heal minor crises or ailments.

According to the Tree of Life, the reality is very different. Our awareness changes because our bodymind changes, and our bodymind changes as a result of becoming more whole — because we are *already* healing. Becoming whole means remembering the power of life, celebrating the unity of nature, and acknowledging the unique qualities within us. We gain greater awareness when the life energy is flowing more freely and effectively in our body; when the energies that were separated finally begin to share their story with the rest of us. This occurs as mechanical tension within our body is released; as tension is released, this alters the biochemical elements that can bind to the surface of our cells. From this change at a cellular level, we gain new or greater awareness.

Each shift in our bodymind produces new thoughts, feelings, and experiences. Each new shift in our consciousness is a reflection of the power of healing. Profound new awareness is a consequence of healing, not the cause. It occurs through a greater expression of the power of life that heals, animates, coordinates, and inspires. The flow of life through our bodymind is a powerful aspect of healing, bringing not only profound awareness, but healing our emotional and physical wounds. The fruits of this kind of healing grow larger, sweeter, and juicier, requiring no picking from the Tree of Life. They simply fall off the tree into our awareness with no effort at all.

Jerry's Story

Jerry had pain in his arm for over sixteen years, and nothing seemed to alleviate it. Finally, after a series of bodywork sessions, he gained greater movement in his neck, his respiration became easier, and he spontaneously began to cry. Jerry had never cried before, and did not even know why tears were streaming down his face. At that time, it felt so good to him that it didn't really matter. A few hours later, he remembered being dragged by that arm from the orphanage to his new foster parents' home, causing him to be separated from his brother against his will. The morning after Jerry had this experience, his pain was gone, never to return. Jerry's wounds were the "cracks" in his personality through which the power of life could finally flow. As the channels for energy and information, respiration and life force, in his body were made available to him, Jerry healed. The fruit fell from the Tree of Life into Jerry's awareness as a result of the healing that had already occurred.

. . . . *HEALING MAGIC* . . . .

Today I choose to eat the fruit of the Tree of Life. I open myself to healing first, knowing that new awareness will follow. Life is the source of all awareness that inspires and empowers me. I know that life itself is the greatest teacher, and for this I am grateful.

· 32 ·

healing myth

Healing involves transcending my past traumas
and negative experiences.

According to this myth, the more we distance ourselves from feelings we do not like in the quest to reach stillness, bliss, and love, the more successful we are on our spiritual path. In this myth, a sweet, nonaggressive disposition is the basis for a healthy life, and expressing anything contrary to this must be avoided. In fact, if the conscious mind could select our experiences in life, all uncomfortable situations would be avoided.

In New Age mythology, the preferred word to describe this experience is *transcendence*. Words like *avoidance, denial,* or *resistance* are typically used in a negative sense. To transcend, meaning to "rise above," implies that enlightenment comes at the end of a spiritual ladder. It is the peak experience we all seek. As we climb the ladder, we pass over any negative past experiences, along with feelings of anger, frustration, and other "unenlightened" states of consciousness.

Transcendence can create miraculous changes in our physiology, but the question is, What is the motive for the transcendence? If it is to avoid what we do not like or want, the outcome will only create further separation from the undesired part or energy. As a result, that energy will build up more tension in order to be set free, which only requires more transcendence. This sets up a pattern of avoidance and denial, as we try to dodge uncomfortable feelings. In contrast, the transcendence of consciousness for the purpose of including all of the bodymind's vibrations and rhythms is a different story, and is likely to produce profound benefits. In this case, transcendence is not based upon avoiding a negative experience, but on attaining a more inclusive state.

The energy or vibration of past traumas and negative experiences needs to be felt and acknowledged by the entire bodymind. Once this occurs, we transform, rather than transcend, the trauma or negative experience. When we experience a trauma, and the higher centers of the brain cannot focus attention on the intense emotional vibration of an experience, it causes the emotional energy that cannot be experienced to be redirected to a particular region of the body. Eventually, the energy in that region must be expressed. If we judge this vibration as a "negative emotion," this only keeps it separated within rigid walls, causing further isolation from the emotion.

Healing occurs when the energy and its vibration are reviewed and experienced by the higher centers of the brain. When this occurs, it liberates the life energy that was being used to build the walls, and it becomes available to heal us. The release of the emotional energy further empowers the healing of our bodymind.

Martin's Story

Martin's brother, Randy, had been abusive to him as a child. Although Martin felt no anger toward his brother as an adult, he sensed that there was something unresolved about his childhood. Then Randy died suddenly. Just a few years earlier, their mother had passed away. After her death, Randy had chosen to avoid his feelings, and devote all his energies to his business so he could retire by the age of fifty. Up to two weeks prior to his passing, Randy appeared aerobically fit and physically strong. In the course of two weeks, he had difficulty breathing and required oxygen to breathe, especially when seated. After a battery of medical tests, he was diagnosed with a late stage of lung cancer.

Randy was told that chemotherapy could extend his life for up to two years. Without chemotherapy, he would have three to five months to live. Randy knew he had to make changes in his life; he decided to undergo chemotherapy because he needed more time to know what changes to make. The day after his first treatment, Randy unexpectedly died at the age of forty-eight.

Martin had a very busy teaching schedule, and was beginning a weekend seminar the day he heard of his brother's passing. He continued to teach the entire seminar, and arrived just in time to attend his brother's funeral. Although Martin felt grief, he had difficulty expressing it, and he maintained a busy teaching schedule over the next few months. When he finally had the opportunity to spend a few days alone and grieve, he went to Las Vegas with a group of friends instead. When he returned home, he buried himself in his work once more.

Six months later, Martin developed pneumonia and acute pain in his chest. Not wanting to stay in bed, he continued to work, socialize, and travel. Eventually, his chest hurt so much that he finally had no choice but to go to bed. He coughed so hard that he had to place his hands on his chest and rub it. Every time he did this, he felt a sense of deep grief for having lost both his mother and his brother. Physical illness often creates the opportunity to receive our body-mind's messages, rather than transcend them. For Martin, his condition helped him to stop transcending the uncomfortable, and gave him permission to more fully experience his pain and grief.

We do not have to transcend our past traumas and negative experiences in order to heal. While transcendence is valuable in life, in healing, the only way out is *through* feeling. Healing requires that we feel the vibration and energy we have kept separate from us, and allow the power of life to work its magic.

· · · · · · · · · · · · · *HEALING MAGIC* · · · · · · · · · · · · ·

All my experiences and feelings have a story to share with me. I accept each story's wisdom, whether or not I enjoy the story. I heal by allowing myself to fully experience all the emotional energies of my being. I observe and participate with different vibrations, without needing to interpret them. All my experiences bear gifts for me, and I gratefully accept them.

· 33 ·

healing myth

I must understand my feelings to heal.

Healing does not require that we learn or understand anything. No matter how much we try to observe, analyze, or study our feelings, it is both tiring and frustrating to find that we never have enough understanding. This frustration is part of the indigestion we suffer when we eat the fruits of the Tree of Knowledge. Understanding our feelings may come spontaneously, but we can heal without understanding them, because feelings are not always meant to be understood.

Donald's Story

My elbow and arm had been very painful for several weeks. They hurt so much that I felt intense pain even when using a light force to touch a patient. Using my arms and hands was part of my identity as a successful chiropractor serving several hundred patients weekly.

One day, I decided to hold my arm and elbow, and look deeply into it as if I was a miniature of myself and could jump right into the area of pain. I shouted to my arm, "What do you want?" Within seconds, my anger and frustration turned to grief. I felt sorrow about something that had happened to me in my childhood, but I didn't know what I was sorrowful about. It seemed that part of me knew the answer, even though I didn't consciously understand what had happened or why. The pain disappeared instantly, and although I felt pain a few more times over the next couple of days, it never returned. By placing my attention on the area calling for my attention, by holding it, and speaking to it as if it was a person in need of help, something happened within me. These actions allowed me to resolve, without any further conscious thought, the energy behind my distress.

Understanding what happened to us, or why we feel as we do, are gifts we are given occasionally as we heal. When we do not search for the meaning of our feelings, but instead observe what we are doing differently, what we desire that is different, or what we are giving that is different, we can embrace our understanding from the Tree of Life. Our feelings may speak to us as gnawing, throbbing, or burning sensations, for example. They may speak to us as comfortable or uncomfortable, as we place attention on them. This is essential for the healing process. As a particular vibration intensifies, and as our ability to place attention on that vibration increases, we cannot avoid being aware of the feeling. As we can feel it, we begin to heal it, and as healing progresses, it becomes easier to feel without having to classify or label what we feel. This is a powerful road sign on the journey of life.

When we cannot avoid a feeling and are overwhelmed by it, it is important to get help from someone who will give us a contextual story for our experience, and a means of accepting what we feel. This can help our bodymind to gain greater flexibility and "make room" for feeling more. At times we may even choose to treat, or cure, our symptom or condition until we feel safe and are ready to receive its gifts.

. . . . *HEALING MAGIC* . . . .

My feeling, not my understanding of my feelings, allows me to heal. The feeling is the message I receive about myself. There are many types of feelings in different parts of me. I allow them to tell me what they want me to know. Through the energy and vibration of my feelings, I receive answers to my questions, inspired by my own ancient wisdom.

· 34 ·

healing myth

One stage of healing is better than another.

In my first book, *The Twelve Stages of Healing,* I have outlined twelve distinct stages that we experience in our healing process. Each stage involves a greater awareness of, and participation with the energy, vibrations, and body rhythms that have been separated, forgotten, ignored, or blocked from free expression. Each stage has a distinct rhythm that imparts its wisdom and unfolds from the healing of the previous stage.

Suffering is the first stage. This occurs when we are confronted with a traumatic or chaotic event or loss, and is characterized by the feeling of absolute helplessness. It is also a stage when we are unable to simply hold a part of our body, breathe into that area, or focus our attention on it.

Stage Two begins with the search for the "magic genie" who will save us from our distress or crisis. We try to gain power over our

helplessness by seeking solutions through external authorities, procedures, or treatments. In Stage Two, we become aware of our rhythms and
polarities, and discover that we are partially responsible for our distress.

In the third stage of healing, we feel that we have "been here
before" and are stuck; we are unable to progress further. At this point,
it is essential not to consider our experience as bad or wrong, but
simply allow it to build up tension and break through into the fourth
stage of healing.

In Stage Four, we initially get angry that we have lost our
power and are determined not to let it happen again. We feel whole
enough to reclaim our power, making choices from the perspective of
"I deserve more than this."

The fifth stage of the healing process involves confronting
whatever it is that kept us separate from our self. With the strength
and wholeness gained through the first four stages of healing, the
fifth stage happens spontaneously and powerfully.

Stage Six involves preparing ourself for change, knowing that
we have learned something profound about ourself in the previous
stage, although we are not yet sure what it is. In this stage of healing,
we gain flexibility, adopt new habits, and feel the restless energy
within us as it prepares to be released from our bodymind.

The seventh stage of the healing process is characterized by
energetic discharge, whether through yelling, vomiting, coughing,
fever, or a loss of something (or someone) in our life. At the end of
this stage, the trapped or stagnant energy is finally gone. As a result,
we feel free, open, and grateful.

In the eighth stage of the healing process, we find ourself saying, "Thank you, thank you," as we are free of the trapped energy that blocked us from connecting with ourself and everything around us. In Stage Eight, situations and events appear to be perfectly timed and divinely ordained to our benefit.

The ninth stage brings an awareness of the life force flowing through us and into the world around us. We become acutely aware of a deep, yet subtle, connection between ourselves and our environment, and begin to perceive life as energy, love, and the light behind all form. This stage of healing is often accompanied by feelings of peace, joy, and awe for the energy that animates our body and our mind.

In stage ten, we are no longer beings filled with light and energy. Instead, we are energy and love itself, in union with all of nature. Immense wisdom is gained during this stage as we lose our sense of self as separate from the world around us, and merge with the wholeness of our being.

In Stage eleven, we generously share with others what we have gained in the healing process. In this stage, we remain in awe of the miracle of life while performing our daily activities. We participate in daily life, without competing with others for attention, energy, or control. Our lives become strongly guided by magical thinking. We know that we have gifts to share with others, and that the world is a magical place of belonging.

As we enter the last stage, that of community, we realize that "we are each other's medicine." We recognize the greatest gift we can give to others is to receive the gift of their presence. Through community, we often encounter difficulty receiving those gifts with gratitude. This places us in a situation where we feel helpless, and we revisit the first stage of suffering, thus beginning the cycle of healing once more.

The key to mastering the wisdom of each stage is to get into its rhythm rather than try to get out of it. The experience of each stage is valid, even if we do not understand it at the moment. Although some stages are more enjoyable than others, none is better than another. Each stage of healing calls upon us to take a risk and move toward wholeness. As we move toward wholeness, we are better able to receive the magical gifts that each stage offers.

. . . . *HEALING MAGIC* . . . .

Wherever I go, there I am. When I am attentive to where I am in the moment, I am magically carried to a new stage of my healing. Because I cannot resolve a situation from the same consciousness that created it, I embrace the stage of healing I am in, and maximize its gifts to me. When I am not in the stage I love, I love the stage I am in.

Epilogue

You are in the presence of an old friend you haven't seen in many years, and the two of you are talking about old times. Suddenly you stop all the chatter and shout, "Yes!" You remember that feeling. Like a pebble being dropped into a still pond, sending ripples of memories through your mind, it is as if the two of you had never parted company. You feel you have come "home" again.

You are hiking through the woods and something compels you to step off the trail. Maybe you are following a chipmunk or a deer, or want to get over a ridge to better observe a rainbow or cloud formation. Perhaps you don't need any reason at all to explore the area that is calling you to share in its glory. As you stand, basking in the sun, watching the vast sky change form as clouds shift in a kaleidoscopic dance of beauty, you call out, "Yes!" Not only are you not embarrassed if anyone else heard you, but you hope that everyone did.

Every cell of your being is awake and alive. Colors seem brighter, sounds seem crisper, and the faint scent of moist pine trees simultaneously flows through your nostrils, taste buds, and brain. Your breath deepens, you are filled with gratitude, and you have a song in your heart. You know you have come "home," and that one day you will return here again.

You and your spouse have been quarreling about an issue you both feel passionate about. At the same time, when you view the issue from a broader perspective, it is meaningless. During the entire discourse about who was right, who was wrong, or why something happened, she grasps your hand as she attempts to make a point. A current runs up your arm and explodes into your heart, softening it. In this moment, you know there is a more important meaning or purpose for your union. You don't even care what it is. You hold her, and gently whisper, "Yes!" With her, you know that no matter where you are, no matter what you do, or no matter how successful you will be at your endeavors, you are "home."

In each of these cases, life energy is pulsating through your bodymind, awakening your senses, and triggering memories of the connection and wholeness we experience as "home." Throughout this book, we have shown that healing involves journeying toward a greater experience of the life energy that animates, inspires, coordinates, and heals. In coming home to healing, there is a series of questions you can ask yourself to help make the transition from the old story of curing your symptom or condition, to the new story of healing your bodymind. These questions are part of the patient survey

I designed for doctors to use in their clinical practice. They are not intended to diagnose disease, but to help the patient discover "the person inside." The person inside is the one who develops conditions and resolves them, as distinguished from the condition itself. Asking yourself these questions may give you a better perspective of your circumstance, and empower the healing process.

In the questions below, you will evaluate whether you have the same health concerns as a family member, regardless of the symptomatic expression. If so, are they truly your concerns and your creation? Did you first experience your concern as your own, or as that of your parents, for example? It is common for people to have similar health concerns as other family members, with or without manifesting similar symptoms. We learn our stories of the world from our family, friends, and mentors. They teach us how to respond to life when we are placed under stress or challenged by unexpected situations.

1. If you have a health concern, have any other family members had a similar concern?

2. What did she do about it?

3. Did it seem to work? What did the treatment "working" mean to her?

4. What was different about her after treatment?

5. What was different about the symptoms after treatment?

6. What was different about her concern about the condition after treatment?

7. What have you done about this health concern?

8. Did it seem to work? What did the treatment "working" mean to you?

9. What was different about you after treatment?

10. What was different about the symptoms after treatment?

11. What was different about your concern about the condition after treatment?

To effectively monitor your own healing process, it is essential to separate the following three things: your symptom, your concern about the symptom, and your assessment of yourself. Rather than asking, "How do I feel?" concerning the symptom, you might ask, "How do *I feel* about how I feel?" referring to the person inside, who is experiencing the symptom and projecting his story onto it. For example, you may have shoulder pain that bothers you, but the pain is not the basis of your concern. Your concern is that you will not be able to play golf as you normally do. For someone else, the concern may be that the symptom is an indication of a more serious disease. For another, the concern may be that she would not perform well in sports or at work. For some, persistent pain is associated with their emotions, while for others, pain is viewed as the lack of motion (or lack of emotion) in a part of their body. Sometimes you may experience pain and still feel okay; there is just the pain. At other times, the pain becomes your focus and major preoccupation. Again, the experience of pain is not as important as "How do *you*, the person experiencing and giving significance to the pain, feel about it?"

Maria was afraid that she might get dizzy if she received any
form of body work, if she played sports, or even if she touched certain
parts of her body. For Maria, feeling dizzy meant feeling the raw emotions of her body, and this signified being out of control. She resisted
the feeling or vibration underlying the experience of dizziness so
much that she would become nauseous. In all the years she had this
problem, she never really vomited, but she was worried that she might.

I remember asking her, "So what would happen if you vomited, or passed out, or your pain got worse. What then?" "Well, oh, I
won't let that happen," Maria would reply. The symptom she experienced had a strong connection to the energy that was alienated from
the rest of her bodymind. The energy took on a physical form as a
symptom that was to be avoided, no matter what. Many people get
dizzy, lose control, vomit, and experience pain. However, Maria's concern about her symptom was not the issue. At issue was the *story* she
had created about the symptom not being allowed in her life.

My clinical experience has taught me that people who just
want to "fix the symptom," and do not wish to discuss their personal
relationship to that symptom (including the life they have lived, or
their concerns about the symptom), often have a powerful disconnec-
tion from an energy that has become separated from the rest of their
bodymind. The symptom itself is rarely the problem. The major concern is tied into the story this person has about the world, and how
she views issues like rapid change, chaos, and not being in control of
her situation.

The very act of acknowledging that our symptom, our concern, and the story behind our concern are separate issues is part of the healing process. When we are "disconnected" from the energy and awareness of our bodymind, all three issues merge into one. As we heal, each of these questions can be addressed individually. Eventually, we are able to separate whether we have just a symptom, or a worry that we will not be able to do something, accomplish something, achieve a goal, or feel what we do not like feeling. Often, the concern is associated with a fear of loss (such as virility, power, spouse, finances), or the ability to work, sleep, or have fun. As our healing progresses, we gain the ability to assess one aspect of our condition without having to reflect upon the other two factors. Usually this is accomplished only after a greater awakening to our body's language, pulsations, breath, and movement.

When we are ready to dedicate ourselves to wholeness, the following questions may help us to further separate the experience of the symptom from the concern, and place it in the context of our daily life. It is interesting to see how life shows us what it needs by helping us to focus on those activities, thoughts, or relationships that may be causing disharmony.

1. How is this symptom or situation altering my work? Play? Rest? Sleep? Relationships? Sex and love life? Concentration? School? Other activities or functions?

2. As time progresses, even if the symptom persists, is there less of an effect in all these areas of my life?

3. If the symptom disappears, are the above areas of my life still affected?

4. Is there any time, activity, or place I can go where I totally, or almost totally, forget about the symptom or the concern itself?

5. Is there anything I do, or any place I go to, that intensifies the symptom or my concern?

The next question will often give us a direct answer that shocks us. First, quiet yourself and gently breathe while touching the part of your body you have concern about. Now ask yourself:

6. Why do I think this has happened or continues to happen to me?

Wait for a response. Then write down anything that comes to you. Keep writing no matter how ridiculous or out of context the answer may be. Know that your bodymind wants you to be healthier and wants you to know the truth. While your answer to the previous question may have truth in it, the next question is even more powerful. Be prepared to have the answer jump out at you.

7. Is this the sole cause of my problem?

Wait a minute or two before you write down your answer. Then ask yourself:

8. If the answer is no, what else is involved?

It is magical to see how asking these questions can put us in the position of honoring the Tree of Life. We are honored in turn by knowing that things are not always as they appear. I once had a patient, who had no knowledge of the body, spirituality, or the role of emotions or stress in health and disease, simply blurt out, "I have cancer because I hated my father and one night I prayed for him to die a terrible death, and a week later he burned to death in his car." It is common for people to spontaneously hold the afflicted part of their body during or after making such a statement. In my patient's case, her bodymind wanted so much for her to ask these questions, and then give herself permission to heal. With that statement, the woman cried almost continuously over the next two days, which further empowered the clinical care I had provided.

To continue to assess your healing, it is important to ask yourself the following questions:

1. If this condition were to go away tomorrow, what would be different about my life? (What would I be doing differently at home, work, play, or in relationships if I did not have this symptom or concern?)

2. Would I have made that change if I did not have the symptom or concern?

3. How else would I have allowed myself to make that change?

4. Have I touched or rubbed a part of my body that I usually do not pay attention to, more, or differently, than before?

5. Have I talked to other people and pointed to this part of my body that I usually do not consider?

6. Have I cried, moaned, dropped to my knees, or fallen in a position that surrenders to my body's rhythms?

7. When was the last time I did that, and what was going on in my life at the time?

8. What would have had to happen in my life to get me to take time to do this?

9. What do I think my bodymind is trying to tell me has to change?

10. What do I need that I am not getting?

11. What do I have to give that I am not giving?

12. Can I truly experience my symptoms, condition, or situation as a gift?

As your healing progresses, this final question is more likely to be affirmative. It is also interesting to notice when the answer shifts from "no" or a *mental* "yes," to a *physical feeling* of "yes." When this occurs, feelings of gratitude may swell up from within, and you may better understand what inspires you to celebrate the healing already in progress, in spite of the outcome you wanted.

Remember, you can heal in spite of the persistence of symptoms or pain. Although your doctor is skilled in knowledge of disease and symptoms, you are the expert about your own health. I encourage you to ask yourself the questions in this chapter every few months to get a sense of how your relationship with your self-healing has deepened. These questions may help you to realize that eventually you must surrender to your biology irrespective of your stories or your psychological state. As you hold yourself and move, breathe, and allow your bodymind to express whatever sound naturally emerges (be it moaning, groaning, humming, singing, or other forms of toning), you feel your internal rhythms, breath, and vibrations as they are, without the need to create a story about them.

As your bodymind heals and attains a greater degree of wholeness, you simply observe your thoughts floating by, without being controlled by them. Instead of paying attention to thoughts that take you into the past or the future, you sanctify your bodymind by paying attention to its present state.

When you sanctify your bodymind, you experience a sense of wholeness, a sense of power, strength, peace, knowing, and gratitude. The power of life flowing through you spontaneously transforms you. Your physiology changes to allow for both healing and your body's own internal curing process, and you stop doing things that distract you from the needs of your bodymind. You come "home" to the energy of your own being, and enter a state of awareness that "knows" beyond all doubt that you are connected to everything around you. You reclaim the power to heal within you, and allow the beauty of healing magic to manifest more fully in your life.

Summary of
Myths and Magic

Social Myths

1

Myth: Healing requires a trained professional or a highly educated specialist.
MAGIC: My healing is natural, spontaneous, and magical. I celebrate the innate wisdom and ability of my body to heal me. I nurture the magical healing power that is mine and mine alone, whether or not I receive the assistance of trained professionals.

2

Myth: Healing is not always available.
MAGIC: Healing is always available to me. The door is wide open for healing to occur in this instant and in the instants to follow. I may choose to be assisted by a health practitioner, or I can initiate the healing process by breathing more fully, touching my body, and allowing it to move freely and express what was formerly repressed. By doing so, my own healing rhythms are set free.

3

Myth: *Healing is expensive.*

MAGIC: The internal process that is mine alone is both priceless and free. Although I may pay for a professional to assist me in regaining my health, the process initiated by me, within me, and through me is absolutely free. I claim my freedom to heal and celebrate my own healing power.

4

Myth: *Healing takes a lot of work and requires full commitment.*

MAGIC: My healing is effortless and natural. My commitment to heal is a natural process requiring no work or special focus on my part. I am grateful for where I am in my healing process. I commit to my wholeness because it feels natural to do so.

5

Myth: *Healing means becoming more balanced, comfortable,*
and in control of my experience.

MAGIC: I give thanks for the unexpected events that take me from my established course and bring new experiences, relationships, and healing. I take this moment to rejoice in the miracle of life. I trust the flow of life, wherever it takes me, and make room in my day to celebrate changes in my schedule and plans. I am nurtured by change, and embrace both chaos and order in my life.

6

Myth: *Healing means understanding what went wrong, or who did what to me.*

MAGIC: To heal, I don't need to understand what has happened in my life or why. I celebrate the miraculous interrelatedness of people, events, and circumstances. I allow myself to experience a new state of consciousness by expanding my chest with air, and placing my hands on my heart. As my body-mind heals, my awareness shifts, and old wounds dissolve into nothingness.

7

Myth: *Someone else has to have healed from this disease before I can do it.*

MAGIC: I am a powerful, creative, and evolving being. The power of life that creates and sustains me knows precisely how to heal me. I give my physiology permission to allow this power to flow through me and to heal me. It is okay for me to be the first to have healed in this way. My healing inspires countless others to trust the healing power within.

8

Myth: *In healing, to be average is normal, and therefore desirable.*

MAGIC: I have no need to be average or normal. I surrender the need to fit into the expectations of others at the expense of my own evolution. At times, upon claiming my wholeness, I may look, sound, or "test" nonaverage. I joyfully celebrate my loss of normalcy, and claim my authenticity, sanity, and health.

9

Myth: *Healing means liking my experience and agreeing with the outcome.*

MAGIC: I love and honor my body, even when I don't like my experience. When physical symptoms or pain arise, I pay attention and accept them without judgment. The messages of my body are perfectly timed for my healing. I listen to the rhythms and messages of my body, and attend to its needs with compassion.

10

Myth: *Healing is a destination.*

MAGIC: My healing is a lifelong journey into greater self-discovery and awareness. I reclaim my personal power, and appreciate my sacred body. I celebrate the power of life that attracts what I need to be whole in body, mind, and spirit. Today, I live my life gracefully receiving the feelings and awakenings of my ever-changing bodymind.

Biomedical Myths

11

Myth: *Every disease or illness can be traced to a physical cause.*

MAGIC: I surrender blaming a single cause for my symptoms, pain, or lack of health. I acknowledge all aspects of my life that may have inhibited or altered the expression of life energy within me. My symptoms and pain remind me of my need to participate more fully in the world. I celebrate and bless the free exchange of energy and information within my bodymind.

12

Myth: *Symptoms and disease are inconvenient "obstacles"*
that need to be controlled or eliminated.

MAGIC: My symptoms alert me that my bodymind needs more self-respect, compassion, and my focused attention. They may require that I spend quality time with myself, or even guide me to change my direction and choices in life. I patiently accept my symptoms as information, vibration, and pulsation, with a story to tell me about my life's journey.

13

Myth: *Healing means symptoms and disease disappear or come under control.*

MAGIC: I accept myself unconditionally, with all my symptoms, conditions, and glorious imperfections. I am healing in spite of the imperfections that still appear in my body and my life. The healing power of my bodymind is more powerful than I ever imagined. As I heal, I experience my whole self, including my light and my shadows.

14

Myth: *If symptoms disappear shortly after treatment,*
the treatment is responsible.

Magic: My symptoms and distress guide me to heal. What worked for me at one point may no longer serve me today. What seemed to hurt me yesterday may be my current remedy. I honor my healing cycles and my participation in a greater plan. The power within me is part of a greater power. I am amazed at how it heals me, in spite of what I consider to be the cause or the cure.

15

Myth: Healing means feeling better.

Magic: I celebrate the totality of my feelings. I celebrate the individual parts of me, and the individual feelings of those parts. I pay attention to my feelings, knowing that their meaning will become self-evident at the perfect time, in the most exquisite way. I celebrate the healing that occurs in a continuous cycle of pleasure, pain, comfort, and discomfort.

16

Myth: A person may be too far gone to heal.

Magic: My present situation is perfect for me. I can heal, regardless of my expected outcome. I hunger to better know the power that resides within me, and the love that I can express. I eagerly express the greatness that I am, and I share my love and greatness with others. I accept my life as a sacred journey that is guided by the power, wisdom, and strength of life itself.

17

Myth: Healing is predictable in its course.

Magic: The information and energy within me is now becoming "whole" again. As I acknowledge the parts of myself that have been ignored, isolated, suppressed, or forgotten, new and surprising insights spontaneously emerge from within me. These lead me to make new choices, help me to transform my relationships, and establish new ones. I joyfully welcome the unexpected outcome of this "new" me.

18

Myth: Healing takes time.

MAGIC: I am healing in this instant. I honor the healing that has already occurred, and I honor the healing that has yet to occur. Healing myself *now* is my gift to myself, to my family, and to my friends. Although my healing is instantaneous, it may take time before I fully experience the benefits.

19

Myth: Healing often requires drastic measures.

MAGIC: I do not have to take drastic measures to heal. The energy that expresses itself as tension, pain, disease symptoms, or an unhappy, unfulfilled life is waiting for the opportunity to burst forth. I am ready to liberate this energy, to set it to work toward healing. I bless my symptoms, illness, and wounds because they are stepping-stones on my healing journey.

Religious Myths

20

Myth: Heaven is only available after this life.

MAGIC: I accept the state of consciousness known as "heaven," while living here and now. I know that my body and my life are sacred here and now. I honor my body and joyfully declare the presence of the Divine as it joins my life here on Earth. Today, regardless of my circumstance or situation, I choose to experience heaven.

21

Myth: Disease is a punishment for my sins.

MAGIC: My symptoms, disease, or circumstance are not a punishment from God. They guide me to pay greater attention to the life force within me, so it can manifest with greater ease. I move forward in my healing, honoring myself and serving others. I rejoice in the fact that spring always follows winter, and give thanks for the healing that has brought me this realization.

22

Myth: *I must forgive in order to heal.*

MAGIC: I am open to forgiveness for myself and for others whenever the timing is right for me. Today, I celebrate the forgiveness that has spontaneously sprung forth in my life, and I honor the healing that has already occurred. For those I have not yet forgiven, I trust that forgiveness will come as my bodymind heals.

23

Myth: *The self or ego is the cause of distress or disease.*

MAGIC: I joyfully acknowledge both my inner "self," and the "me" I see in the mirror. I smile as I realize that little of what I thought was "me" is true about myself. I celebrate who and what I am, and who and what I am not. I reclaim my new sense of "self," my identity, and renew my passion for healing by saying "yes" to life.

24

Myth: *The days of prophecy are over;*
messages from the divine are not available to me.

MAGIC: God communicates with me in many ways. I receive divine messages through my dreams, intuition, and relationships with others. Divine messages may appear as sound, light, images, and emotion. In faith, I receive messages that are broadcast from the Divine. I rejoice in the communications I am given, and celebrate the gifts received through experiences that deviate from my usual patterns and routines.

25

Myth: *Uninhibited expressions of the human body*
are not as sacred as religious prayer.

MAGIC: I celebrate the union of body and spirit. Through movement, breath, and the compassionate touching of my body, I gain insight into myself. By sanctifying my body, I open the door to healing. I take time out from all my activities, preoccupations, or thoughts, to honor my body and to pray a new and ancient prayer to my Creator's gift to me.

26

Myth: *Silence will heal me.*

MAGIC: Nature helps me to heal, whether it is noisy or silent. I may prefer to retreat from noise and activity, or I may choose noise and activity to activate my healing. I am grateful for the many ways in which the power within me uses noise within the stillness, and stillness within the noise to heal me. I can heal in any environment, because nothing exists outside of nature.

New Age Myths

27

Myth: *I am responsible for creating my reality.*

MAGIC: I am not responsible for creating my external reality. I am responsible for my internal state of mind, emotion, and vibration. I am responsible for focusing my attention on my inner environment in relationship to my life circumstances. It is my gift to become aware of the state of tension, pain, or ease in my bodymind, and to accept my experiences — pleasant or unpleasant — with nonjudgment and love.

28

Myth: *I must "open my heart" in order to heal.*

MAGIC: I celebrate the participation of all physical, energetic, and spiritual centers of my body. I place my hands on each center, gently breathe into each area, and experience my body rising and falling in that region. My body resonates with love for every part of my bodymind, and broadcasts this energy through my being and into the world.

29

Myth: *Being highly evolved means no longer having negative emotions.*

MAGIC: I evolve as I become aware of the different parts, energies, and relationships of my bodymind. I heal as all of my parts share their stories with one another without judgment. I transform as I experience the energy and tension that has been isolated and ignored. There is no such thing as a "negative" emotion; there is only information and energy that is now made available for me to heal.

30

Myth: *People who are "enlightened" do not experience disease.*

MAGIC: I am becoming aware of my internal energies, rhythms, feelings, and thoughts. Greater joy and enlightenment are a bonus of this awareness. I regard my symptoms and disease as a gift with valuable lessons to share with me. Being present with, and accepting all of my gifts, is the path to enlightenment.

31

Myth: *Profound new awareness is necessary in order to heal.*

MAGIC: Today I choose to eat the fruit of the Tree of Life. I open myself to healing first, knowing that new awareness will follow. Life is the source of all awareness that inspires and empowers me. I know that life itself is the greatest teacher, and for this I am grateful.

32

Myth: *Healing involves transcending my past traumas and negative experiences.*

MAGIC: All my experiences and feelings have a story to share with me. I accept each story's wisdom, whether or not I enjoy the story. I heal by allowing myself to fully experience all the emotional energies of my being. I observe and participate with different vibrations, without needing to interpret them. All my experiences bear gifts for me, and I gratefully accept them.

33

Myth: *I must understand my feelings to heal.*

MAGIC: My feeling, not my understanding of my feelings, allows me to heal. The feeling is the message I receive about myself. There are many types of feelings in different parts of me. I allow them to tell me what they want me to know. Through the energy and vibration of my feelings, I receive answers to my questions, inspired by my own ancient wisdom.

34

Myth: *One stage of healing is better than another.*

MAGIC: Wherever I go, there I am. When I am attentive to where I am in the moment, I am magically carried to a new stage of my healing. Because I cannot resolve a situation from the same consciousness that created it, I embrace the stage of healing I am in, and maximize its gifts to me. When I am not in the stage I love, I love the stage I am in.

ABOUT THE AUTHOR

Donald M. Epstein was born in Brooklyn, New York on December 7, 1953. After attending Brooklyn College, he received his Doctor of Chiropractic Degree from New York Chiropractic College in 1977. Through his keen insight into the healing process, he developed Network Spinal Analysis and Somato Respiratory Integration. His groundbreaking work has been the subject of numerous articles and research papers throughout the world, and has inspired the academic community in a wide range of disciplines.

Dr. Epstein has trained thousands of individuals in his innovative healing techniques. His first book, *The Twelve Stages of Healing*, published in 1994, has been translated into five languages. He currently travels around the world with his wife, Jackie, leading healing intensives and training seminars, and delivering public lectures. He lives in Boulder, Colorado.

For information about healing intensives and training seminars, Network Spinal Analysis, or Somato Respiratory Integration, please contact:

Innate Intelligence, Inc.
444 North Main Street
Longmont, Colorado 80501

Phone: (303) 678-8086
Fax: (303) 678-8089

http://www.DonaldEpstein.com
http://www.InnateIntelligence.com

The Twelve Stages of Healing by Donald M. Epstein with Nathaniel Altman
This book takes us beyond traditional books on healing by identifying twelve basic rhythms or stages of consciousness common to all of humanity. Each stage imparts its wisdom and unfolds from the healing of the previous stage. Powerful exercises and declarations help us to maximize our healing experience.

The Way Toward Health (A "Seth" Book) by Jane Roberts
Seth Speaks about the mechanics of self-healing and the influence of the mind upon our physical health. The last book ever dictated by Seth, and never before published.

Living Without Limits by Deepak Chopra & Wayne Dyer (Audio cassette)
Two leaders in the field of human potential share their wisdom before a live audience as they question and challenge one another on the importance of quieting the inner dialogue, the power we have to heal ourselves of fatal diseases, the negative impact of the media on our health, and more.

The Seven Spiritual Laws of Success by Deepak Chopra
In this classic bestseller, Deepak Chopra distills the essence of his teachings into seven simple, yet powerful principles that can easily be applied to create success in all areas of our life. (Also available in Spanish, and on audio cassette.)

Make Your Dreams Come True by Pamala Oslie
With simple games and processes, this book takes us on an exploration of the thoughts and beliefs that unconsciously rule our lives, then shows us how to change those beliefs to make our dreams come true.

ALSO FROM AMBER-ALLEN PUBLISHING

The Angel Experience by Terry Lynn Taylor
Bestselling author, Terry Lynn Taylor, gently guides us to cultivate a deeper relationship with the angels in our everyday lives. Each chapter includes practice ideas that encourage a life filled with grace, wonder, and humor.

The Four Agreements by don Miguel Ruiz
Based on ancient Toltec wisdom, The Four Agreements offer a powerful code of conduct that can rapidly transform our life to a new experience of freedom, true happiness, and love. (Available in Spanish as *Los Cuatro Acuerdos,* and on audio cassette, read by actor Peter Coyote.)

The Mastery of Love by don Miguel Ruiz
Using insightful stories to bring his message to life, Ruiz shows us how to heal our emotional wounds, recover the joy and freedom that are our birthright, and restore the spirit of playfulness that is vital to loving relationships.

Available at Bookstores Everywhere
or call toll-free (800) 624-8855

For a free catalog of our books and cassettes, contact:
Amber-Allen Publishing, Inc.
Post Office Box 6657
San Rafael, California 94903-0657
Phone: (415) 499-4657 • Fax: (415) 499-3174

Visit our website:
http://www.amberallen.com